Roy Umble

1973

Seattle

Readers Theatre:
Toward a Grammar of Practice

Consulting Editor:

DON GEIGER

University of California, Berkeley

Readers Theatre
TOWARD A GRAMMAR
OF PRACTICE

Joanna Hawkins Maclay

University of Illinois

Random House   New York

Readers Theatre: A Grammar of Practice

JOANNA HAWKINS MACLAY

Copyright © 1971 by Random House, Inc.
All rights reserved under International and Pan-American Copyright
Conventions. Published in the United State by Random House, Inc., New
York, and simultaneously in Canada by Random House of
Canada Limited, Toronto.

Library of Congress Catalog Card Number: 70–127550

Manufactured in the United States of America.

Composed by Cherry Hill Composition, Pennsauken, N.J.

Printed and Bound by Halliday Lithograph, Inc.
West Hanover, Mass.

First Edition

9 8 7 6 5 4 3 2 1

Designed by Ronald Farber

PERMISSION   ACKNOWLEDGMENTS

Acknowledgments are gratefully extended to the following authors and publishers for their kind permission to quote from copyrighted material.

Rudolph Arnheim, *Art and Visual Perception: A Psychology of the Creative Eye.* Copyrighted 1954 by the Regents of the University of California. Reprinted by permission of the University of California Press.

Lawrence Durrell, "The Alexandria Quartet." From the book *Justine* by Lawrence Durrell. Copyright © 1957 by Lawrence Durrell. Reprinted by permission of E. P. Dutton & Co., Inc. and Faber & Faber Ltd. From the book *Balthazar* by Lawrence Durrell. Copyright © 1958 by Lawrence Durrell. Reprinted by permission of E. P. Dutton & Co., Inc. and Faber & Faber Ltd. From the Book *Mountolive* by Lawrence Durrell Copyright © 1958 by Lawrence Durrell. Reprinted by permission of E. P. Dutton & Co., Inc. and Faber & Faber Ltd.

Lawrence Durrell, "Bitter Lemons." From the book *Bitter Lemons* by Lawrence Durrell. Copyright © 1957 by Lawrence Durrell. Reprinted by permission of E. P. Dutton & Co., Inc. and Faber & Faber Ltd.

Lawrence Durrell, "Prospero's Cell." From the book *Prospero's Cell* by Lawrence Durrell. Copyright © 1960 by Lawrence Durrell. Reprinted by permission of E. P. Dutton & Co., Inc. and Faber & Faber Ltd.

Lawrence Durrell, "Letters." From the book *Lawrence Durrell: Henry Miller: A Private Correspondence,* edited by George Wickes. Copyright © 1962, 1963 by Lawrence Durrell and Henry Miller. Reprinted by permission of E. P. Dutton & Co., Inc. and Faber & Faber Ltd.

Lawrence Durrell, *An Irish Faustus,* Scene Six. From *An Irish Faustus* by Lawrence Durrell. Copyright © 1963 by Lawrence Durrell. Reprinted by permission of E. P. Dutton & Co., Inc. and Faber & Faber Ltd.

Lawrence Durrell, "Alexandria." From *Collected Poems* by Lawrence Durrell. Copyright © 1956, 1960 by Lawrence Durrell. Reprinted by permission of E. P. Dutton & Co., Inc. and Faber & Faber Ltd.

Lawrence Durrell, "Bitter Lemons," "Exile in Athens," "The Anecdotes: XIV, In Rio," and "Cities, Plains and People (Part I)." From *The Poetry of Lawrence Durrell.* Copyright © 1956, 1960 by Lawrence Durrell. Dutton Paperback Edition (1962). Reprinted by permission of E. P. Dutton & Co., Inc. and Faber & Faber Ltd.

Flannery O'Connor, "Everything That Rises Must Converge." Reprinted with permission of Farrar, Straus & Giroux, Inc. from *Everything That Rises Must Converge* by Flannery O'Connor. Copyright © 1961 by the Estate of Mary Flannery O'Connor.

Dylan Thomas, "Adventures in the Skin Trade," from Dylan Thomas, *Adventures in the Skin Trade and Other Stories.* Copyright 1955 by New Directions Publishing Corporation. Reprinted by permission of New Directions Publishing Corporation and David Higham Associates, Ltd.

For Robert S. Breen

Contents

Readers Theatre:
Toward a Grammar of Practice

chapter one

Introduction

Theatre may be defined as a medium characterized by two features: a text and a performance. When we look at this definition in the light of contemporary theatre practice, we can see that the relationship between the two elements is such that the performance is the dominant feature in most theatrical presentations. On the other hand, a need has frequently been voiced for another kind of theatre—a theatre in which the *text* would be featured.

Almost since its inception, Readers Theatre has been committed to the principle of featuring, with a special kind of clarity, literary texts. This clarity is sometimes obscured in conventional theatrical productions. By "featuring the text," I mean that the purpose of the production is to clarify, illuminate, extend, or provide insights into the particular literary text being presented. Too often, however, "text" has been reductively defined as "words." Such a definition tends to ignore the fact that the correct vocal utterance of the text's words, enveloped in appropriate emotional tones, does not necessarily result in featuring the text in a performance. Such a definition also tends to disregard the fact that the presence on stage of the physical text (a book, manuscript, or any form of printed words) does not necessarily result in featuring the text as a form of human experience.

Although it is true that most Readers Theatre directors have a set of principles that serve as guides in directing a Readers Theatre production, one is not always sure how these principles correspond to the particular literary text being presented, or, indeed how these principles serve to *feature* the text. If all of the performers on stage are holding manuscripts and directing their lines toward the audience, these techniques may signal to a certain segment of the audience that this is "Readers Theatre"; however, the mere presence of a manuscript on stage or the placing of a scene "out front" will no more feature the literary text than will getting rid of the scripts and placing a scene "on stage." Such techniques as "out front scene placement" and the presence of a manuscript on stage will not in themselves serve to feature or clarify a literary text or to increase insights into the particular text.

The obvious questions to be posed at this point are: (1) What, then, is this text that is to be featured in Readers Theatre, if it is not "words"? and (2) How is this text to be featured in Readers Theatre, if not through the physical presence of the manuscript on stage? In answer to the first question, a text is certainly composed of words. But, more important, it is *more* than words. Words are the *means* through which the action or experience within the text is expressed; they serve as a means of presenting to the mind and senses of the auditor the total experience (realistic and imaginative, explicit and implicit, detailed and suggestive) of a text. The text's words are neither its action nor its experience; its vitality and life are dependent upon the sensitive reader, who can make the necessary extensions and perceive the necessary manifestations of paralanguage, nonverbal language, gesture, and so forth, which are inherent in the text, but which the words in themselves cannot express. If Readers Theatre is to feature the text as defined in these terms, it seems specious to reason that such a purpose will be accomplished simply by placing the manuscript of the text on the stage. Instead of posing the question, "What can we do with the book?" it seems more purposeful to ask, "Does the presence on stage of a manuscript of this text create any particular effect and, if so, can the presence of the manuscript be utilized in this production to illuminate some psychological or aesthetic aspect of the text?" The shift in emphasis in these questions applies with equal vigor to other traditional features of Readers Theatre.

Readers Theatre has traditionally been interested in presenting a literary text with a special kind of simplicity and a minimum of theatrical trappings. Somewhere along the line, certain accompanying principles evolved, apparently in the interests of featuring the text, which have come to be associated with Readers Theatre. These techniques usually involve the use of manuscripts, the use of lecterns or reading stands, the delivery of lines in a presentational manner, and the minimizing of physical action, costumes, scenery, and properties. On the other hand, throughout this country, in recent years, more and more, Readers Theatre directors have been breaking with tradition by asking a reader to handle more than one role, putting a scene on stage rather than out front, and so forth. However, while these breaks with traditional Readers Theatre practice are readily observable, the rationale behind the break is often baffling. Too often a director's decision to break with tradition is based on his intuition rather than on any clear understanding of how such a break relates to the particular literary text that he is presenting.

If Readers Theatre is to fulfill its original function of featuring the literary text, then more than tradition and intuition are needed to serve as guides. A grammar of practice is needed— a body of aesthetic principles that are directly related to the relationships among the performers, the audience, and the text —principles that will serve as guides in the task of featuring the literary text in a performance. There are certainly ample source materials on conventional theatre and traditional Readers Theatre that are readily available to those interested in featuring a special kind of *performance*. But if a body of principles that will allow the performance to serve the literary text is being sought, rather different kinds of sources will have to be consulted, such as the evidence provided by the history of theatre practice, the history of literary structure, the psychology of visual perception, and the history of aesthetics.

This book is an attempt to *begin* filling the need for an aesthetic for Readers Theatre by abstracting from such sources some principles of audience-text-performer relationships. The book is written primarily from the point of view of the Readers Theatre director; it considers particular problems encountered by the director and suggests how the abstracted principles of audience-text-performer relationships could be applied in a production that is aimed at featuring the literary text. Chapters Two through Six consider problems encountered in selecting literature, and in casting, directing, and designing; there is also a brief discussion of performing in Readers Theatre. Chapter Seven provides practical application of the principles discussed by taking a complete Readers Theatre script and indicating how these principles could be used to feature the text in performance.

chapter two
Selecting Literature

The first step for any director in the theatre is the selection of the script. For the director in the conventional theatre, this job is somewhat simplified, because he usually chooses a play. There is nothing in the definition of theatre, however, that limits it to the presentation of plays. Indeed, Kenneth Tynan has suggested that theatre is "anything exciting that happens in a darkened auditorium on a lit stage—lectures, tub-thumping, dance, mime, whatever."[1] If Readers Theatre is defined as a technique for staging literary texts in such a way that the text is featured in the performance, then it seems logical to assume that any literature, by virtue of its being literature, is available for consideration as a Readers Theatre presentation —not only plays, but also novels, short stories, histories, biographies, travel books, letters, diaries, journals, essays, lyric poetry, epic poetry, social documents—indeed, the whole range of literary expression.

Plays are obviously the most readily available material for Readers Theatre, because most plays are written with the performance in mind. The director is thus relieved of the burden of compiling a script to a length suitable for an evening's performance. There is, however, another value in using plays for Readers Theatre. When the conventional theatre's current emphasis on the *performance* of a text and Readers Theatre's emphasis on the *text* in performance are compared, it becomes evident that a Readers Theatre treatment of certain plays could provide new insights into the structure or texture of plays that conventional staging might tend to obscure. One example can be found in the history of the Broadway and the road company productions of Voltaire's *Candide.* The lavish Broadway musical, resplendent with elaborate settings, costumes, and other spectacular accoutrements, was not very successful. Some critics complained merely that it was "too beautiful"; others sensed that Voltaire had gotten lost somewhere in all the theatrical trappings. When the show went on the road, in what was billed as a "concert version," the original script was retained, but the technical apparatus was stripped to essentials. As a result, the characters became clearer, their complex interrelationships became more apparent, and Voltaire's satirical commentary emerged as vividly as it does in the printed script. To the surprise of many, the road show production was quite successful.

Perhaps an even better example can be found in Shakespeare's *Titus Andronicus.* A very interesting combination of executed action and described action characterizes this early play of Shakespeare's. Enacted scenes of blood and gore (such as Titus' feeding the human pie to Tamora) are juxtaposed with described scenes of blood and gore (such as Marcus' description of Lavinia's ravishment). In a Readers Theatre presentation of this play, which would be interested in featuring the text of the play, close attention would be paid to those scenes that create their effect through one's *seeing* the horror as opposed to those whose effect is created through one's *hearing* the horror described by one of the characters. In a Readers Theatre treatment of *Titus Andronicus,* the director's decision concerning which action to stage fully and which not to stage will be determined by the text of the play, not by a principle that all action should be staged fully (as is sometimes the case in conventional theatre) or by a principle that no action should be staged fully (as is sometimes the case in traditional Readers Theatre). Hopefully, such a presentation of *Titus Andronicus* would make clearer certain aspects of the play's structure and texture, which could not be guaranteed by traditional staging techniques. Such a close following of this play could lead the audience to realize some of the play's weaknesses and this, too, it should be noted, is a valuable function that Readers Theatre can perform. By presenting a literary text in its completeness, exposing its weaknesses as well as its strengths, Readers Theatre has the potential of serving as a valuable critical device for the study of literature.

Although most plays could probably profit from the special treatment given them in Readers Theatre, it seems a shame to overlook or ignore the abundance of nondramatic literature (that is, non-plays) in existence. Non-plays do present a practical consideration—the limitations that must be imposed when a performance must be contained within one evening. But many short stories, and some long poems, such as Byron's *Childe Harolde's Pilgrimmage*, are approximately the same length as a conventional play. The director simply has to assign the lines to the performers (which, it is granted, can sometimes be the major part of his preparation).

Although it is true that most literary texts will not read like neat ninety-minute packages, length should not deter the director from considering any work of literature. The presentation of relatively long or short works can be achieved in a special kind of program, the composite program, which can be one of the most interesting kinds of Readers Theatre productions. Such a program also has the virtue of providing additional critical insight into the literature, through the nature of the entire program and the relation of the individual selections or parts to the whole program. One kind of composite program consists of a long work that has been carefully cut and edited to fit the limitations of a performance that lasts for an evening. A careful cutting of Stephen Vincent Benet's narrative poem *John Brown's Body* or Truman Capote's novel *In Cold Blood* could possibly clarify or illuminate such aspects of the literature as its point of view, plot structure, or character relationships. Equally important is the consideration that such a program makes available to audiences literature (such as novels) that would otherwise not be seen in the theatre.

Because of the special nature of narrative literature, the

aesthetic and practical problems encountered in adapting this literary form to the stage are many and varied. These problems have been explored extensively by Robert S. Breen through the development of what he has called "Chamber Theatre."[2] Chamber Theatre is a technique for presenting narrative literature on the stage in its original form and staging it in such a way that the text is featured. There is no essential difference between Chamber Theatre and Readers Theatre as we have defined it; Chamber Theatre is Readers Theatre whose literary text is in narrative form. It should be noted that the terms will be used interchangeably in discussions of staging narrative literature.

Another type of composite program combines several separate works into a unified program. One of the added values of this kind of program is the extra dimension of understanding and appreciation that is possible through the very combination of the several works. For example, in one Readers Theatre production, which featured selections from the works of Lawrence Durrell—his plays, novels, letters, poems, essays, and travel books—what emerged for the audience, in addition to the experience of the individual texts, was a real sense of Durrell himself, the man and the artist. In another program, featuring modern Southern writers, the company presented three individual stories—William Faulkner's "My Grandmother Millard and General Bedford Forest and the Battle of Harrykin Creek," Eudora Welty's "Petrified Man," and Flannery O'Connor's "Everything That Rises Must Converge." An important part of the audience's experience with such a program was, obviously, the experience of the individual stories. But the total experience for the audience involved an additional dimension—an understanding of the South, gained through seeing three different points of view and attitudes toward the South taken from three different periods of history (the Civil War South, the South of the 1940s, and the South of today). From the program emerged an understanding of the complexity and the continuity of the South that probably would not have developed with the presentation of only one story.

The possibilities for composite programing are limitless. A Readers Theatre production of "Swift's Masks," for example, might include several of Jonathan Swift's essays in which he utilizes personae to effect his satirical purposes. Such a program could clarify not only the character of the individual personae in A *Modest Proposal, Argument Against Abolishing Christianity, The Drapier's Letters,* and *The Battle of the Books;* it could make quite vivid the similarities and differences in the various personae, as well as Swift's methods of satire.

The composite program might also focus on a city, such as Alexandria, Egypt. For such a program, a variety of sources is available, ranging from such nonfictional works as E. M. Forester's *Alexandria: A History and a Guide* and Henry Miller's correspondence to more imaginative literature such as the poetry of C. P. Cavafy and Lawrence Durrell's tetralogy of novels, *The Alexandria Quartet.* Indeed, one such program, which took London as its focus, provided the audience with three Londons in one: the Londons of Samuel Johnson, Charles Dickens, and Virginia Woolf.

A controversial issue could also be the core of a program. Such a program might present a composite of the views of several leading writers on the subject. It might take the Civil Rights issue and utilize writings by James Baldwin, Ralph Ellison, Langston Hughes, P. D. East, Harry Golden, and so forth. The list of possibilities could go on and on; in fact, there are more possibilities for this kind of programing than there is literature in existence.

There is no necessity, then, for Readers Theatre to limit itself to plays, or even to literature that is sometimes called "dramatic" (that is, literature involving at least two clearly delineated characters engaged in a readily discernible conflict). The director in Readers Theatre never has to feel at a loss for literary material. With the wealth of literature available and the ingenuity of a trained critical imagination, a director can find Readers Theatre to be a most exciting medium in which to work. Readers Theatre, because it takes all of literature as its province, opens the door to an endless variety of literary and theatrical experiences, for directors, actors, and audiences alike.

chapter three
Casting

Once the Readers Theatre script has been selected, the next order of business is casting. In conventional theatre, this is a relatively simple (although sometimes frustrating) problem. A play's dramatis personae lists a certain number of male and female characters, and the director chooses one actor to portray each character, usually attempting to cast as close as possible to the character's physical type.

But why must there be an exact correlation between the number of actors and the number of characters? and why typecast? The history of theatre practice shows that such has not always been the case with casting. Many instances can be found in which the ratio of the number of actors to the number of characters was not one to one. Paul Baker's famous production of *Hamlet*, for example, used several actors to portray the title character. The Greek theatre and some of August Strindberg's chamber plays, on the other hand, often used fewer actors than there were characters in the plays. Often Readers Theatre productions use a small number of actors to portray a larger number of characters. Although this method of casting is frequently dictated by the limited number of available actors (for example, where would the director in a small liberal arts college find enough actors to play all the roles in *War and Peace*?), such casting methods can reveal more psychological and aesthetic truths about the performed literature than conventional casting does. In a production that does not adhere to a one-to-one ratio between actors and characters, the presence of one actor playing a number of roles emphasizes the similarity in his roles; on the other hand, the presence of more than one actor playing one character emphasizes the differences within the character. Because Readers Theatre takes its principles from the text being performed rather than from conventional theatre practice, there is no necessity for an exact correlation between the number of actors and the number of characters. Indeed, an astute director can use the principles of multiple casting to provide the audience with new insights into individual characters and character relationships in a given text.

There are numerous ways in which a director might use one actor to play several roles. For example, one actor might play roles with similar character traits, such as a miser and a man who is stingy with his affections. One actor might play characters who have a similar social status, such as all of the Italian peasants in Alberto Moravia's *Two Women,* or all of the messengers in Sophocles' *Theban Cycle.* In addition to these instances, one actor could be used to play characters who have a similar function within a certain literary work, such as all of the women who contribute to the protagonist's downfall in J. P. Donleavy's novel *The Ginger Man.* In one Readers Theatre production of James M. Barrie's *Peter Pan,* the director made a most interesting use of this principle of multiple casting. The same three young men were used to play the Darling brothers, the Lost Boys, the Indians, and the Pirates. Although their characterizations of the Darlings were quite distinct from their characterizations of the Lost Boys, and both were quite distinct from their characterizations of both the Indians and the Pirates, the use of the same actors to portray each group of "boys" allowed the audience to recognize the characters' similarities more readily than would have been possible with conventional casting.

In addition to using one actor to portray several characters, the director can also use more than one actor to portray one character. Such casting could provide an excellent means of illuminating the psychological divisions in a character such as Deborah Blau, the schizophrenic protagonist of Hannah Green's novel *I Never Promised You a Rose Garden*. Double casting of this sort could also illuminate the temporal distance and the shifting psychological distance between the "narrating I" and the "experiencing I" in William Carlos Williams' "The Use of Force." This principle could also be used to underline part of Richard Brinsley Sheridan's comic technique in *The Rivals;* two actresses could be used to contrast the public and private behavior of Mrs. Malaprop. In a production of Eudora Welty's "Why I Live at the P.O." in which two actresses were used to portray the narrator-major character, Sister, the double casting not only clarified the bifurcation in Sister's personality, but it also allowed the audience to see and hear two different Sisters: Sister the paranoid postmistress who tells the story, and Sister as she sees herself—a Cinderella figure who is mistreated and persecuted by her family. The double casting in this production also provided the audience with a visual dramatization of the dialogue being conducted within the mind of Sister, a young woman who is constantly *reminding herself* of imagined wrongs that have been committed against her.

Theatre history shows not only that a one-to-one relationship between characters and actors has not always existed, but also that typecasting has not always been the rule. Indeed, men and women have not always played men's and women's roles, respectively. Although the practice of casting men in women's roles may have been a matter of necessity for the Elizabethans (just as it is for the director in a boy's school today), a principle emerges from this practice that can be applied to Readers Theatre: The presence of male actors playing female characters, or vice versa, tends to emphasize the dual or ambivalent sexual nature of the character. That is, the audience sees a male actor creating the illusion of a female character, and it sees both sexual natures simultaneously. It is probably no accident that Shakespeare's romantic heroines are quite "boyish," since Shakespeare was writing for a theatre in which the heroines were played by boys. In the contemporary theatre, also, some productions of *Peter Pan* have used an actress to play the title character, and in so doing have emphasized Peter's youth (or undefined sexuality), his femininity as well as his boyishness. In one Readers Theatre production of A. A. Milne's *Winnie-the-Pooh* stories, an all-girl cast portrayed the animals and Christopher Robin. Such casting in this case tended to "desex" the otherwise boylike characters, and to create a clearer illusion of universalized "children and animals," such as Milne so skillfully manages to create in his text. This principle could be applied, however, in works where the ambivalent sexual nature is not so apparent or is a motivating factor in the text's conflict. A man playing Hedda Gabler, for instance, would no' doubt tend to underscore Hedda's masculinity, as well as illuminate her latent homosexuality.

A combination of the casting methods discussed so far might also be utilized to achieve another kind of effect in Readers Theatre. For example, if two actors, a man and a woman, were used to portray Hedda Gabler, the casting might provide more insight into the play than could be achieved by using either one man or one woman, because the casting could dramatize more fully the internal conflict of Hedda as well as the various manifestations of this conflict with the different characters, such as Thea, Judge Brack, Lovberg, Tessman, and Aunt Julia.

The director in Readers Theatre, then, does not necessarily have to adhere to the conventional one-to-one relationship between the number of actors and the number of characters when casting his production, nor does he have to typecast. He should, however, recognize the aesthetic and psychological principles at work in multiple casting. With these principles as his guide, he is capable of providing actors and audiences alike with many insights into the complexities of character functions and character relationships in literature.

chapter four
Directing

Preliminaries

Having chosen a script and assembled a cast, the director now turns to the major job of directing the Readers Theatre production. His first task is the interpretation of the text. He has already been engaged in interpreting the text to some extent, of course, during the course of casting his production, and even in selecting or adapting a script. For instance, in cutting Edgar Lee Masters' *Spoon River Anthology* to a suitable length for an evening's performance, the director has not cut at random; his interpretation of the text has influenced his decision to cut certain poems, retain certain poems, provide transitional material, and so forth. If he does not use conventional casting techniques, his interpretation of the text has determined his decision to cast more than one actor for a particular role, to cast one actor in several roles, and so forth.

Once the script and the cast are selected, however, the director moves on to larger areas of textual interpretations, so that he and the cast are clear in their mutual understanding of the text's theme and tone. The director of Renoir's scenario *Grand*

Illusion, for example, must make clear to his cast that he understands the theme to be that the idea that "all men are brothers" is the Grand Illusion. The director of a comedy such as *The Merchant of Venice* would have to make clear to the cast that the tone is comic, not tragic or sentimental, and he would have to specify what *kind* of comic tone he understands the play to manifest. The actors in Readers Theatre will have to know the director's interpretation of these overall aspects of the text, because their performances will be determined by the director's decisions regarding theme and tone.

Staging

Although the director has to some extent engaged in a rudimentary interpretation of the text during the preliminary stages of his production plans, his staging of the production is the most important way in which he interprets the text. In a very real sense, the Readers Theatre director's staging of a text *is* his interpretation of the text. If he is attempting, through the performance, to feature the experience of a particular text, then his staging must serve to fulfill the wholeness of that text. Every piece of blocking, every bit of business, every suggestion to an actor will have to be determined by the specific text with which he is working.

SCENE PLACEMENT

A basic consideration for any director is the placement of action, or the direction in which lines of the script are delivered. Let us begin with the notion that every literary work assumes a reader or listener. In Readers Theatre, the audience is essentially in the position of this silent reader, and the text is on stage. This reader-listener, then, comes to experience the text either by being *told directly* or by *overhearing.* If we look at the history of theatre practice, we can see that these literary effects have also had their counterparts in theatrical staging. We can see a parallel between being told directly and the use of asides in the Elizabethan theatre, the neoclassical French theatre, and the Restoration and eighteenth-century English theatre, whereby a character would turn to the audience and address them directly. On the other hand, probably the most obvious example of the "overhearing" effect occurs in the late-nineteenth- and early-twentieth-century "fourth wall" realistic theatre, where the audience is supposedly absent and is over-hearing the lines and viewing the action from a position some-what like that of a Peeping Tom. The principle which seems to evolve from these practices is that the direction of lines toward the audience (or "out front") tends to emphasize the effect of being told directly and to negate the sense of overhearing; the direction of lines away from the audience (or "onstage") tends to emphasize the sense of overhearing and to negate the sense of being told directly. In Richard Brinsley Sheridan's *The School for Scandal,* this effect is spelled out in the text in the scene where the disguised Sir Oliver walks through Charles Surface's gallery, interrogating Charles. When Sir Oliver asks about a portrait of himself, we "overhear" him telling Charles, "But, sir, I have somehow taken a fancy to that picture"; but when Sir Oliver exclaims, "The rogue's my nephew after all!"[1] we are clearly to be told this directly. This example seems obvi-ous enough, but let us look at the following passage from Eudora Welty's "Why I Live at the P.O.":

"So that's the way the land lies," *says Uncle Rondo. There he was, piecing on the ham.* "Well, Sister, I'll be glad to donate my army cot if you got any place to set it up, providing you'll leave right this minute and let me get some peace." *Uncle Rondo was in France.*

"Thank you kindly for the cot and 'peace' is hardly the word I would select if I had to resort to firecrackers at 6:30 A.M. in a young girl's bedroom," *I says back to him.* "And as to where I intend to go, you seem to forget my position as postmistress of China Grove, Mississippi," *I says.* "I've always got the P.O."

Well, that made them all sit up and take notice.[2] [Italics added.]

This passage illustrates a device that is particularly important to the way in which we receive the experience of this story. We move back and forth from the illusion of overhearing the characters converse with each other, to the confrontation of Sister speaking directly to us, as in the italicized phrases. This effect in the story could be accentuated through the staging by having Uncle Rondo and Sister talk to each other during their dialogue exchange and having Sister speak the italicized lines directly to the audience. Either having Sister speak everything toward the audience or having her speak everything away from the audence might tend to obscure this particular effect in the text.

Both of the examples cited so far seem rather clear in their intended effects of overhearing and direct telling. Let us now consider the following dialogue exchange between Algernon and Jack in Oscar Wilde's *The Importance of Being Earnest*. Here, the effect is not quite as obvious:

Jack: My dear Algy, I don't know whether you will be able to understand my real motives. You are hardly serious enough. When one is placed in the position of guardian, one has to adopt a very high moral tone on all subjects. It's one's duty to do so. And as a high moral tone can hardly be said to conduct very much to either one's health or one's happiness, in order to get up to town I have always pretended to have a younger brother of the name of Ernest, who lives in the Albany, and gets into the most dreadful scrapes. That, my dear Algy, is the whole truth pure and simple.

Algy: The truth is rarely pure and never simple. Modern life would be very tedious if it were either, and modern literature a complete impossibility!

Jack: Literary criticism is not your forte, my dear fellow. Don't try it. You should leave that to people who haven't been at a University. They do it so well in the daily papers.[3]

While this passage seems, on the surface, to be a simple dialogue exchange between the two men, it is also quite apparent that not only are we meant to overhear their conversation, but also to be told certain things quite directly. Notice the difference, for instance, between Jack's "You are hardly serious enough," which is certainly meant for Algernon, and Jack's "When one is placed in the position of guardian . . . ," which is certainly intended as much for the audience as it is for Algernon. By the time the exchange about literary criticism is reached, it seems clear that Jack and Algernon are not talking to each other so much as they are engaged in an amusing piece of rhetorical commentary aimed directly at the audience. The Readers Theatre director, then, might well utilize the "over-hearing versus direct telling" principle in his staging to feature this particular quality in the scene.

Looking at this same passage from *The Importance of Being Earnest*, we might also say that the dialogue shifts from particularities to generalities. That is, Jack's remark about "the whole truth" concerns a particular truth, whereas Algy's rejoinder is a generalization about the nature of Truth. The suggested staging of this scene, in which Jack would direct his line to Algy and Algy would address his line to the audience, would also tend to underscore this contrast between the particular and the general. The second principle of staging, then, is that: The direction of lines toward the audience, or the delivery of lines in a presentational manner, tends to universalize, or generalize, the experience; the direction of lines toward the characters on stage, or in a representational manner, tends to particularize the experience.

Support for this principle can be seen in several areas of theatre history, but perhaps the clearest example can be found in the Greek theatre, particularly in the structure and staging of tragedy. From all we can ascertain about the staging of Greek tragedy, it appears that the choruses usually delivered their lines in a presentational manner, directly to the audience; furthermore, these choruses were used not as participants in the particular conflicts of the characters, but as "sounding boards," who frequently generalized the feelings of the characters or of the spectators. The application of this principle to a Readers Theatre production could serve well to elucidate a text that is characterized by a shift from particularized repartee between characters to highly generalized remarks by the characters. Through the application of this principle, a sense of the essentially epigrammatic character of the dialogue of a text such as *The Importance of Being Earnest* could be made even more immediate for the audience than it would be in a more conventional theatre treatment. Indeed, one Readers Theatre production of Shakespeare's *Cymbeline* used these principles of line delivery and managed to convey to the audience not only the very moving experience of the action, but also a particular quality of the structure of the play—the constant shift back and forth from representational to presentational manner and from particularities to generalities.

These principles of line placement can be utilized, of course, not only in plays, but in any form of literature where these effects may be present. In the following passage from J. D. Salinger's novel *The Catcher in the Rye*, for example, note how the italicized sections seem to indicate a generalized comment, whereas the unitalicized sections seem to focus on particulars:

The thing is, though, I liked Old Morrow's mother. She was all right. "Would you care for a cigarette?" I asked her.

She looked all around. *"I don't believe this is a smoker, Rudolph,"* she said. Rudolph. *That killed me.*

"That's all right. We can smoke till they start screaming at us," I said. She took a cigarette off me, and I gave her a light.

She looked nice, smoking. She inhaled *and all,* but she didn't wolf the smoke down, *the way most women around her age do. She had quite a lot of charm. She had quite a lot of sex appeal, too, if you really want to know.*

She was looking at me sort of funny. "I may be wrong, but I believe your nose is bleeding, dear," she said, all of a sudden.[4] [Italics added.]

This balance between specific detail and generalized commentary, which is clearly characteristic of the style of Holden Caulfield, the narrator-major character, could be demonstrated in a Readers Theatre production through application of the staging principles discussed here.

One final principle or effect should be mentioned, which is more or less a corollary to the two principles discussed above. The character who removes himself from other characters and/or speaks lines to the audience speaks those parts of the text not intended for the other characters to hear. Whether these lines are for his ears only (as in a soliloquy) or for a specific listener (as in the speeches of a confidant, or in an aside), the effect is achieved by his withdrawal from the rest of the characters. This withdrawal may be done with his whole body (that is, by the character moving to another part of the stage) or with his voice and the focus of his body (that is, by the character directing his lines to the audience or away from the other characters). Historically, this principle has been abstracted from the French theatre's use of the confidant, the seventeenth- and eighteenth-century drama's use of the aside, and the Elizabethan soliloquy. But the principle could be applied in Readers Theatre not only to soliloquies and asides in plays, but also to interior monologues in narrative fiction. Molly Bloom's internal soliloquy in James Joyce's novel *Ulysses* and the interior narration of Benjy in William Faulkner's *The Sound and the Fury* are cases in point.

Such methods of line and character placement as those described then, take their cues from the text and can therefore serve the director in clarifying or illuminating certain aspects of the text in a way that arbitrary principles, such as the placement of all lines out front or on stage, could not. Because these methods have a particular literary text as their ultimate guide, they override staging principles that are designed primarily to feature a particular kind of performance.

MOVEMENT

Having explored some possible criteria and principles of line placement, let us now turn to a consideration of some problems involved in blocking and stage movement.

Most traditional Readers Theatre principles for stage movement specify a minimal amount of movement and blocking. Conventional theatre principles of blocking generally involve such considerations as "weak" and "strong" areas on stage, and "stage picture"; the latter is in the interest of a pleasant composition of the visual aspects of the performance. These principles, however, do not have much to do with helping the Readers Theatre director translate the experience of the text into a theatrical situation. The Readers Theatre director may well find that a beautiful stage composition parallels a particular aesthetic effect in a text he is staging; he may well find, too, that a minimal amount of blocking serves to illustrate some aspect of the text he is staging. Finally, however, he must be more concerned with quality than with quantity, because his major concern is to ensure that the visual effects in Readers Theatre either parallel, contribute to, or in some way support the experience of the text he is staging.

Because of the Readers Theatre director's peculiar problem in staging, we shall turn to some aesthetic principles and theories based on the psychology of visual perception, and we shall explore the ways in which some of these principles could be applied to staging a text in Readers Theatre.

Let us begin with a theory of movement in visual terms, which takes account of movement in immobile objects and which treats the human figure (actor, dancer, and so forth) as an object in an environment.[5]

If we take at face value the ideas that the strongest visual appeal to attention is motion and that "happenings" attract us more spontaneously than "things," it would be hard to argue for any kind of theatre other than conventional representational theatre. But Rudolph Arnheim's theories of visual perception conclude that an object that truly engages our attention (and especially the attention of the artist) is one whose visual pattern exhibits strong tension, even though the forces that created the tension may have little relation to those forces that they convey to the eye.[6] He says:

Movement of shape presupposes that the artist conceives of every object as a happening rather than as a static piece of matter, and that he thinks of the relationship between objects not as geometric configurations but as mutual interaction.[7]

If there can be movement without motion and objects are indeed "happenings" rather than "things"; if visual perception is not a recognition of static properties, but a reflection of the invasion of the organism by external forces that upset the balance of the nervous system; if the work of art is a dynamic organization of directed tensions, then we are prepared to embrace a theory of theatrical staging based on these principles, which allow it to be a dynamic organization of directed tensions, just as is the literary work of art.

Arnheim further suggests that:

. . . we do not see happenings as such, but rather we see things undergoing change. . . . Any visual object is a dynamic event and . . .

a thing at rest is one in which forces are not absent but in balance. The difference between the immobile shape of a painting or a statue and the body of a dancer in motion becomes secondary.[8]

The paradox or the ambiguity of the trick of nature suggested here by Arnheim applies significantly to movement in Readers Theatre. If the eye apparently sees concrete objects, but no less truly perceives patterns of forces that are not available to the eye (since they are invisible), then how do we unify our impressions—those that are concretely evident and those that are interpretatively abstracted from the visual evidence? It is, of course, through the creative imagination. In the conventional representational theatre, where the relationship between things seen and forces felt is lifelike, the possibility for a unified vision of things and happenings is severely limited. But it is quite possible in Readers Theatre to increase enormously the imagined vision of both things and events, if the evidence presented to the eye is minimized and severely selected, and if reliance is placed on the evidence unseen. If this change in emphasis disappoints some spectators, it may be due to the actor's or the director's ignorance of some of the laws of motion.

Because this study is meant to be suggestive rather than all-inclusive, it shall be limited to a consideration of five major aspects of visual perceptions: distance, motion, velocity, causality, and obliquity.

Let us look, first, at the creation of spatial relationships in the theatre. As Arnheim points out, "The space of a theatre is defined by the motor forces that populate it. . . . Distance is created by actors withdrawing from each other." [9] In the conventional theatre, the space of the stage is framed by a proscenium, and the actors relate to each other along lines that run from one side of the proscenium frame to the other. Under these circumstances, the proportion of the actor to the size of the physical stage is fairly fixed, and the distance created by withdrawing actors is limited to what can happen within those proportions. But let us suppose that the axis of the stage space runs from the stage out into the audience, as is traditionally characteristic of Readers Theatre. In this case, the proportional ratio is infinitely expandable, and there is really no limit to the distance that can be created between two actors-characters. Suppose we have a scene in which one character is waving good-bye to another character who is departing on a train that is moving out of the station. With an axis of stage space running perpendicular to the proscenium, it is possible for the actor on stage to wave good-bye out front to the other actor who withdraws up stage and exits. The actor on stage can remain standing still while the imagined actor and train are disappearing out front. The motor forces at work on the stage, and those available through the spectator's eyes, are represented in the amplitude of the waving gesture of the concrete actor as he stands on tiptoe to make himself larger, so that he may be seen at the great distance that separates him from the actor on the train. The seen actor's volume and pitch will reinforce the perspective.

In conventional theatre, because the proportion of the actor's size to the proscenium frame is relatively fixed, it is awkward to have the reaction of the departing actor expressed simultaneously. Suppose the character in the station is brokenhearted at the departure of his loved one. Suppose the loved one is actually quite relieved to be going away but conceals his relief out of consideration for the lover's feelings. Once the train is sufficiently far away from the lover's close scrutiny, he feels free of this obligation and can express his relief in a relaxed contentment. If the axis of the stage space ran perpendicular to the proscenium, it would be possible in Readers Theatre to have the departing actor sitting next to the waving actor. Such staging would minimize the audience's attention on the actors' overt movements away from each other yet minimized movement is not a virtue in itself in Readers Theatre. What is more important is the fact that we can now see both the illusion of departure and the expression of each character's emotional response to the departure. The distance perspective protects the departing actor-character from observation by the waving actor, while allowing the audience full view. An example such as this shows how Readers Theatre techniques and principles could provide the theatre with a new dimension and perspective that could conveniently accommodate the drama of simultaneity at great distances. Furthermore,

techniques such as the one described might prove quite valuable in illustrating the tension in narrative fiction between the
written text (which must present experience serially) and the
action in the text (whose experience may be characterized by
simultaneity).

Returning to the scene concerning the character who departs
on a train, we might also discuss the implications of the staging
of this scene in terms of Karl Duncker's law of motion. The law
states: "The experience of visual motion presupposes that *two*
systems (figure and ground) are seen as displaced in relation
to each other."[10] That is, we see a cat (figure) as one system in
relation to the floor (ground), a second system, and we see
them in such a relation to each other that displacement occurs.
There are three displacement relationships that are possible:

1. The cat is displaced in relation to the floor.
2. The floor is displaced in relation to the cat.
3. Both cat and floor assume a share in the displacement.

Duncker has formulated a psychological principle that is
directly related to the criteria by which we "see" one system
move and the other system remain fixed. First of all, "in a visual
field, objects are seen in a hierarchic relationship of dependence."[11] Sometimes this dependence is based on size and
motion. For example, the flea seems to be displaced on the dog,
not the dog on the flea. At other times, the displacement is
determined by the "spontaneous organization of the field."[12]
The desk, for example, serves as ground for the typewriter;
the typewriter serves as ground for the typing paper, and so
forth. According to Duncker's rule, displacement occurs in
such a situation by the framework or ground remaining
immobile and the dependent object or figure tending to move.
When no dependence exists, the two systems may move sym-
metrically and at the same velocity.

The observer himself, however, may also act as a frame of
reference. In this event, the movement in displacement may
depend on which object he chooses to fixate. Our actor
departing on the train, for example, will find that if he fixates
the train, it will seem to move over the ground; but if he
fixates the ground, it will seem to move under the train. The

implications are even more interesting for the audience member. On the conventional stage, the stage itself is the frame of reference, and distance is created within the frame as the actors move away from each other or as one moves away from the other. In Readers Theatre, because the audience member is, hopefully, in a position similar to the silent reader of a text, he becomes the frame of reference, and the illusion of movement will depend on the object he fixates. If he fixates on the departing actor, as he perhaps tends to do because the departing actor is the moving object, he may well be under the illusion that he (the spectator) is moving away from the actor standing still on stage.

Duncker's law of motion provides us with a principle of movement that is dependent on relationships—the relationship of two systems. One application of the principle, on the simplest level, is: The illusion of displacement can be created by moving one unit within a relationship. When the axis of the stage runs from one side of the proscenium to the other, the relationships are relatively fixed and distance created is fairly lifelike and fixed; consequently, the amount of displacement created is fairly fixed. When the axis is shifted so that it runs perpendicular to the proscenium, and the actors relate along this line, the illusion of a maximum degree of displacement can be created with a minimal amount of actual movement. The important feature of this principle for the director to remember is that one actor must serve as ground, the other actor as figure. The director will have to understand which character apparently moves a great distance, and which one seems to remain relatively fixed, if this mobile-immobile relationship is important in the text. On the other hand, if the object of displacement is ambiguous in the text, the manner of staging, such as was suggested in the scene of the actor departing on the train, could demonstrate this ambiguity by allowing the audience, as the frame of reference, to choose whether to fixate on Actor A, Actor B, or the widening gap of space between them.

We perceive motion not only in terms of simple displacement. We may well perceive, in the manner of the displacement, certain *qualities* of the ground or the figure or both. In the first place, what could be "objectively" described in terms of velocity, we invariably perceive "subjectively." For example, the same air (objectively speaking) seems to exhibit different qualities when the objects moving through it are a jet plane and a kite. We might say that, in the latter situation, the air seems denser than in the former. Or, we might say that the kite seems to be "battered about" by the air, which seems somewhat "aggressive."[13] When we apply this principle to Readers Theatre, we find that the director's close attention to the velocity relationship of "ground" and "figure" or "container" and "contained" will allow him to demonstrate important qualities in a text that simple principles of stage movement might not allow. The most obvious and general application of this principle lies in the manner of each actor's general movement, in expressing the "tonic" or general personality and temperament of his character. The audience will not simply perceive that two actors move and gesticulate with different speeds; the audience will also assign certain qualities to these movements. A character's slowness, deliberateness, or tiredness can be demonstrated by an actor who is seen moving slowly in relation to an actor who either moves rather fast or remains immobile. The reverse, of course, can also be true. Furthermore, if the text demands it, the actors can express contrasting qualities with a minimum amount of overt movement, thereby allowing the audience to focus on the qualities of the movement rather than the quantity of it.

The following passage is from Flannery O'Connor's "Everything That Rises Must Converge." Let us see how these principles of velocity perception might be applied in a Readers Theatre staging of the scene, in order to illuminate certain qualities of the characters and their environment:

She leaned forward and her eyes raked his face. She seemed trying to determine his identity. Then, as if she found nothing familiar about him, she started off with a headlong movement in the wrong direction.

"Aren't you going to the Y?" he asked.

"Home," she muttered.

"Well, are we walking?"

For answer she kept going. Julian followed along, his hands behind him. He saw no reason to let the lesson she had had go without backing it up with an explanation of its meaning. She might as well be made to understand what had happened to her. "Don't think that was just an uppity Negro woman," he said. "That was the whole colored race which will not longer take your condescending pennies. That was your black double. She can wear the same hat as you, and to be sure," he added gratuitously (because he thought it was funny), "it looked better on her than it did on you. What all this means," he said, "is that the old world is gone. The old manners are obsolete and your graciousness is not worth a damn." He thought bitterly of the house that had been lost to him. "You aren't who you think you are," he said.

She continued to plow ahead, paying no attention to him. Her hair had come undone on one side. She dropped her pocketbook and took no notice. He stooped and picked it up and handed it to her but she did not take it.

"You needn't act as if the world has come to an end," he said, "because it hasn't. From now on you've got to live in a new world and face a few realities for a change. Buck up," he said, "it won't kill you."

She was breathing fast.

"Let's wait on the bus," he said.

"Home," she said thickly.

"I hate to see you behave like this," he said. "Just like a child. I should be able to expect more of you." He decided to stop where he was and make her stop and wait for a bus. "I'm not going any farther," he said, stopping. "We're going on the bus."

She continued to go on as if she had not heard him. He took a few steps and caught her arm and stopped her. He looked into her face and caught his breath. He was looking into a face he had never seen before. "Tell Grandpa to come get me," she said.

He stared, stricken.

"Tell Caroline to come get me," she said.

Stunned, he let her go and she lurched forward again, walking as if one leg were shorter than the other. A tide of darkness seemed to be sweeping her from him. "Mother!" he cried. "Darling, sweetheart, wait!" Crumpling, she fell to the pavement.[14]

Looked at realistically, this scene contains a great deal of overt movement that covers quite a range of distance. Furthermore, the movement is continuous; Julian's mother is ostensibly moving down the street throughout most of this passage. But notice that O'Connor has chosen to place the emphasis in the scene not on the literal movement down the street, but on the characters' conditions at the time. It is only when Julian and his mother finally face each other toward the end of the passage that the emphasis is on their physical activity. If we were to stage this scene so that Julian and his mother move across the stage, around the stage, and so forth, covering an expanse of actual stage space, their overt movement, because it would be large and dynamic on the stage, would take the focus in the scene. How, then, do we realize the story's emphasis *and* its total environment? We can say, first of all, that Julian's mother must create the illusion of moving away from Julian. This can be created in the manner we suggested earlier, if we have the actress playing Julian's mother face away from Julian, out front, and move *in place* along an axis that runs from the stage into the audience. If Julian then relates to his mother along the proscenium line, the illusion is created not only that he is pursuing her, but also that he is "digging in" at her, which is indeed the effect of his verbal attack. Her lack of acknowledgment of him also finds reference in the text. Let us suppose that the actress playing Julian's mother moves with heavy, lurching movements, which are slowed down from a "normal" tempo, and that her body seems in a state approaching collapse. Let us then say that Julian does cover some space on stage as he paces beside her with quick, jerky steps, almost military in fashion (step left, stop, step right, stop, and so forth). The contrasting velocity in the actors' movements will not simply operate realistically, but will also underline an important aspect of the psychological or emotional tone of the characters' relationship. Julian and his mother are moving in two different worlds, just as they seem to be moving through two different media; neither is making contact with the other, either physically or psychologically. In the suggested staging, their manner of physical movement parallels their psychological conditions. At the point where Julian takes his mother's arm and finally confronts her, if the two actors cease their "stylized" movement and actually confront each other on stage, we are prepared to share Julian's experience of shock on its realistic level, without sacrificing the psychological context so vital to the experience.

The preceding illustrations are essentially concerned with overall or general physical and psychological qualities of the characters in a scene, or with the contrasting qualities of characters, which can be demonstrated through contrasting velocity in the actors' movements. The principle, however, can also apply to a scene in which another kind of quality (phasic rather than tonic) is implied in the text. Let us look at such a use of the velocity principle, which is somewhat more imaginative, but which will serve to clarify an important aspect of the text. Instead of thinking of the medium in which the action takes place as something physical (like the water for the fish, which sometimes seems like air, and at other times seems like oil), think of it as a psychological or emotional context. In the following passage from Albert Camus' novel *The Stranger,* note that the context is psychological (the character's emotional state), but the text's medium is verbal (the character's language):

I couldn't stand it any longer, and took another step forward. I knew it was a fool thing to do; I wouldn't get out of the sun by moving on a yard or so. But I took that step, just one step forward. And then the Arab drew his knife and held it up toward me, athwart the sunlight.

A shaft of light shot upward from the steel, and I felt as if a long, thin blade transfixed my forehead. At the same moment all the sweat that had accumulated in my eyebrows splashed down on my eyelids, covering them with a warm film of moisture. Beneath a veil of brine and tears my eyes were blinded.

Then everything began to reel before my eyes, a fiery gust came from the sea, while the sky cracked in two, from end to end, and a great sheet of flame poured down through the rift. Every nerve in my body was a steel spring, and my grip closed on the revolver. The trigger gave, and the smooth under-belly of the butt jogged my palm.[15]

There are a couple of rhythms operating in this passage that a change in velocity of action could clarify in terms of quality. There is, for instance, an alternation of images between those that are concretely realistic and those that are poetically imaginative. The alternation is rapid, but the tempo within the images is slow, or legato. Notice, for example, the verbal repetition for a single act: "I couldn't stand it any longer, and took another step forward. . . . But I took that step, just one step forward."[16] He took one step in reality, but he took three steps verbally. What he did psychologically could be interpreted as, "I took one step out of the sun, I took one step toward the Arab, and I took one step toward my fate as the murderer of the Arab." He took three steps in one. If the actor in Readers Theatre were to take only one step on stage but were to slow down the action as though he were moving through a denser medium than air, he might be able to demonstrate the psychological importance of the experience. The denser medium is not physically identified for the spectator, but it is psychologically identified for him in the density of the language; this is accomplished in this example through repetition. The *action* is a physical step, the *context* is the psychological state of the character who is taking the step, and the *text, or medium,* is language. By changing the velocity of the action, we have changed the quality of the context. Our reason for changing the velocity is found in the medium, or text, of language, which suggests, by its use of repetition, three steps instead of one. What the actor does is to elongate one step, since that is all the character actually takes, into three times the duration, in order to maintain the illusion of slow motion created by the repetition in the language. The principles of velocity and visual perception discussed so far seem to be precisely what Readers Theatre needs if it is to express the character in Camus' novel. That is, in a novel such as this, staging principles have to be based on a complex, agile aesthetic that will allow us to appreciate the subtle relations between the physical and the imagined—between the inner and outer forms of human experience.

Duncker's law of motion also suggests that the perception of motion will be determined by the relative strength of the factors involved. When "the dominant framework is without motion, any immobile object [within it] will be visually perceived as being outside time, just as the framework itself. But when the framework is in motion, the stillness of any dependent object will be interpreted dynamically as either being deprived or incapable of motion or actively resisting displacement."[17] A rock in the midst of a rushing stream, for example, appears to be offering stubborn resistance to the water. The application of this "framework in motion" principle in Readers Theatre can achieve some interesting effects. Suppose Character A is watching with delight Character B being tossed up in a blanket by the other characters. Actor A and Actor B are sitting on stage, facing the audience. A is watching B out front and following the displaced figure up and down with his eyes. The framework in motion is, of course, the blanket in the hands of B's tormentors. The immobile object is Actor B clinging stiffly to his chair with his eyes tightly shut. Actor A is watching an imagined situation of Character B moving up and down in the air, and so too is the spectator. But the spectator also sees Actor B in the role of Character B sitting motionless on the stage. The dramatic effect is that of an immobile figure in a moving-ground framework, and therefore the spectator not only imagines the scene of the moving blanket, but more importantly the audience interprets Character B as "being deprived or incapable of motion or actively resisting displacement."[18]

In addition to motion, displacement, velocity, quality, and resistance, we should also note those principles by which we visually perceive causality. Causality, like velocity, displacement, and other aspects of movement mentioned thus far, may be perceived not on the basis of practical testing, but exclusively on the basis of perceptual conditions.[19] The general condition may be stated as follows:

Causality is perceived when the objects are sufficiently distinguished from each other to appear as not identical and when at the same time the sequence of their activities is sufficiently unified to appear as one unitary process. When these prerequisites are fulfilled, the perceptual force inherent in the primary object is transmitted to the secondary object.[20]

But, says Arnheim, "A slight interval of rest at the moment of contact will break the continuity of the movement and eliminate the experience of causality."[21] Thus, a wooden ball rolling across a screen toward a luminous disk seems to give a push to the disk if the disk begins to move in the same direction as the ball at the moment of contact.

When we apply this principle to staging, we can see that causality does not have to exist literally on the stage in order for causality to be perceived by the audience. But the conditions for the perception of causality must be present. We can also see that if causality is an important aspect of a particular action, the audience must perceive not only the action, but also the continuity of stimulus-response, which constitutes the conditions of causality.

Let us consider the scene in Shakespeare's *King Lear* in which Gloucester's eyes are put out. In conventional theatre staging, this action would be placed on stage; in traditional Readers Theatre productions, this scene would probably be placed out front. Decisions by directors in these cases, unfortunately, usually rest on prejudice toward a particular kind of staging, rather than on the acknowledgment of principles of causality perception. It would not be difficult to imagine a spectator objecting to the staging of this scene in traditional Readers Theatre fashion, in which Actor A makes a two-fingered poking gesture toward the audience, and Actor B, sitting next to him on stage, blinks his eyes and retracts his head with a muttered oath, as if his eyes had been poked. The spectator would object because the cause and effect relationship can be destroyed when the actors do not physically meet in these reciprocal gestures. Actor A's stimulus does not seem to be the direct cause for Actor B's response. Yet according to the principle of perceived causality, it could be possible to place the action out front and create the illusion of causality. The illusion can be created if these two conditions are fulfilled:

1. The gesture and response are well enough timed so that the action seems to be continuous from A to B.

2. The actions of the two actors are directed toward a point in the audience where they seem to meet, and this point of intersecting action has previously been established during the performance.

In this last condition, A and B have been seen to relate along an axis that runs perpendicular to the proscenium, and they have established a triangle; the base of the triangle is the space on stage between the actors, and the illusion of action can be created by having their gesture and response occur at a point somewhere in the audience that represents the apex of that triangle—the point where their two lines of directed action intersect at the moment of the blinding. If these two conditions are met, so are the prerequisites for casuality set forth above.

Obviously, the conditions for casuality could also be met if the scene was placed on stage. If it seems more in the interest of the text to place the action on stage, then it should be placed on stage. What is gained, then, by placing the blinding of Gloucester out front? For one thing, the degree of violence can be stepped up to whatever level is necessary for the scene, because the practical necessity for avoiding actually putting out Actor B's eyes does not have to be considered when the scene is placed out front. When Gloucester is blinded on stage, the actor cannot afford to sacrifice his own eyes, no matter how dedicated he might be. The audience does not doubt causality when the scene is placed on stage, because it has sufficient evidence from the collateral action of the other characters and the screaming of Gloucester, but the action itself will have to be concealed. The Readers Theatre staging suggested above, then, has the added advantage of allowing the audience to see the full intensity of the character's act, without sacrificing the eyes of the actor. The audience can be as thoroughly convinced of the blinding of Gloucester, but the means are much more economical, and the audience can concentrate more completely on the significance of the action.

Let us consider finally the relation of obliquity to the perception of movement. Obliquity is perceived as a deviation from a basic vertical and horizontal framework; the greater the angle of deviating lines, the greater is the movement that is perceived. Arnheim finds a good illustration of the obliquity principle in the windmills of a Dutch landscape, as shown in Figure 1.[22] In Figure 1, windmill A appears to be standing

Figure 1

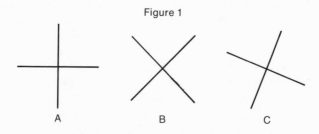

A   B   C

still; windmill B appears, to a slight degree, to be moving and windmill C definitely appears to be moving. In the conventional theatre, there is a tendency for movement to be static, as in windmill A of Figure 1. In traditional Readers Theatre, where a formal relationship between characters is established in the angle of their address as they face the audience, the effect is similar to that of windmill B, as can be seen in Figure 2. In

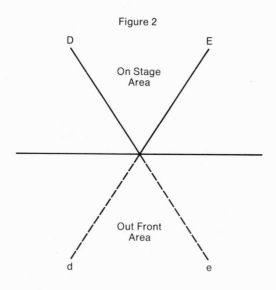

Figure 2

Figure 2, D and E are characters on stage; d and e are the imagined characters out front. In conventional theatre, then, the angle of character relationships tends toward windmill A of Figure 1 and is less dynamic than is traditional Readers Theatre, where the angle of relationships approaches more nearly that of windmill B in Figure 1. Yet windmill C in Figure 1 is the most dynamic and the most likely to stimulate a perception of movement. It is hoped that the Readers Theatre director, under the influence of the principle of obliquity, will shift the angles of relationships, in order to take advantage of the full range of possibilities for achieving different stages of movement from relative stasis to dynamic obliquity.

Now that a number of ways have been suggested in which Readers Theatre can apply laws of visual perception to the staging of literary texts, it becomes clear that Readers Theatre can manifest more motor behavior than conventional theatre, because the imagined behavior, specifically directed so as to seem to contain a whole set of activity, is freer, more extensive, and more carefully directed than is generally possible in either the strictly representational productions of the conventional theatre or the strictly presentational productions of traditional Readers Theatre.

Alienation

The suggested Readers Theatre staging of the scene from *King Lear* has the advantage of allowing the audience to concentrate on the significant action without worrying about the safety of the actor, because the audience is made aware of the simultaneous presence of character and actor. In other words, if the illusion that the two *characters* make contact is successfully created, the audience maintains that illusion while at the same time recognizing that the two *actors* do not literally come into physical contact. Such a condition is similar to what Bertolt Brecht called the "alienation effect"[23] and is the final consideration for our discussion of directing in Readers Theatre.

The term "alienation," as used by Brecht in the Epic Theatre, has no pejorative connotations. It implies a particular kind of detachment that allows certain elements of a dramatic presentation to stand out and that consequently allows the audience to take a critical position. The point of the alienation effect for Brecht was to make the audience think—to make them critical. Theatre was not a medium for emotional catharsis; it was to be a stimulus for social action and social criticism. His theatre was not a representational theatre as such. Erwin Piscator, Brecht's director in the Epic Theatre, encouraged the actors to cultivate an alienation attitude in rehearsals, by having them refer to themselves in the third person and narrate their own stage directions.

We have maintained throughout this discussion that Readers Theatre's primary interest is in featuring the literary text and that staging techniques in the interest of featuring the text may not be representational. We have further maintained that Readers Theatre techniques, because they serve to feature the text, can be a valuable kind of critical tool for the study of literature. It is in this respect that the alienation effect can be most valuable to the director, because the process of Readers Theatre constitutes, in a very real sense, a special kind of literary criticism. Acknowledging the actors as *actors* frees the audience to concentrate on the experience of the text, and (strangely enough) it allows for a fuller illusion of the reality of the literary experience than is often possible in conventional representational theatre. When this alienation effect is successfully managed, the audience can become as emotionally involved in the experience of the characters as the text demands: Their awareness that actors are actually portraying the characters frees their imaginations and sharpens their critical faculties, so that they are in a position both to let the text affect them emotionally and to discover critical insights into the text. In the scene discussed earlier, for example, wherein Character B was tossed in a blanket while Actor B sat tensely still, Character B's mobility and Actor B's immobility constitute Brecht's condition of alienation perfectly. Furthermore, the audience has the double experience of the mobility of the character's frame and the immobility of the character's psychological resistance to the movement.

An illustration of the kind of insight made available through alienation occurred in a production of some stories from A. A. Milne's *Winnie-the-Pooh*. In this production, the cast played children who were being told the stories, which they in turn acted out with the storyteller, at times following the stories in their own books, at times listening to the storyteller, and when the occasion called for it, donning an animal costume and making quite a point of acknowledging, "Now I'm going to play Piglet" (or one of the other animals). A small boy in the audience was so taken up by the experience, yet so apparently unaware of the effect of the alienation, that his remarks shifted back and forth from "I want Winnie-the-Pooh to be my friend" to "When will it be my turn to play Winnie-the-Pooh?"

Let us consider one final and somewhat more complex illustration of alienation, and the stages or degrees of its employment in Readers Theatre. We will consider a scene from Bertolt Brecht's *The Private Life of the Master Race* for which slides are projected on the back wall of the stage or on a screen set up at the back of the stage. Now let us look at several different conditions for alienation in this scene:

Condition One: The characters are on stage giving a Nazi salute and are shouting *"Sieg Heil"* as they face the audience. But the image of Hitler is projected on the screen behind them. Because it is a still picture, the audience will recognize that it is not in truth Hitler himself; but will the audience not be drawn into the illusion that the characters who are ignorant of the picture behind them may indeed be looking at the real Hitler, or at least a real picture of Hitler in some mass parade or meeting in Berlin? Under this condition, the audience is in the position of being saluted as a collective Hitler, and they therefore will sense some evaluation of their position; but because they are looking at a picture of Hitler on the back wall of the stage, they will not feel altogether sure of their position. The audience here is also in the position of a crowd facing the image of Hitler. Consequently, the alienation is created for the audience because of *their* double position. The double position is prevented from becoming split, however, because it is easy to respond to the image on the screen as a mirror reflection of what the characters are seeing out front.

Condition Two: Now the characters on stage turn their backs on the audience and face the image of Hitler on the screen while they give their Nazi salute and shout *"Sieg Heil."* Under these circumstances, the characters are in the same condition as the audience, and both characters and audience are saluting a real picture of Hitler. This condition can be very convincing, since the actual Nazis saluted actual pictures of Hitler at state occasions. Unlike Condition One, there is no double position for the audience, and the degree of alienation is consequently reduced. The illusion of reality, however, is increased, or, at the very least, simplified and concentrated.

Condition Three: Now the image of Hitler is removed from the screen and no projections are used. As in Condition One, the characters salute and shout while facing the audience.

Under these circumstances, the audience find themselves in the position of the imagined figure of Hitler himself (or the imagined picture of Hitler), and they enjoy the uncomfortable position of being elevated to the situation of the dictator himself.

Condition Four: This is essentially a variation of Condition Three, in which no projections are used. As in Condition Two, the characters turn their backs on the audience, saluting and shouting upstage, as though the imagined figure or picture of Hitler were upstage. The audience now is in the same position as the characters, feeling themselves to be swelling the crowd of Nazi saluters and shouters.

Condition Five: A *motion* picture of Hitler reviewing the troops is projected on the screen upstage, as the characters salute and shout facing the audience. There is so strong an impression of alienation that the effect is almost comic. The audience is less likely to believe that they are watching the same thing as the characters. The motion picture prevents the illusion of a reflected image being thoroughly established, since one does not think of a moving image as a reflection as readily as one does a still picture. One tends to think of a motion picture as the thing itself, and one does not generally regard it as merely a picture. This degree of alienation encourages absurdity, because the position of the characters is strained and the position of the audience is disturbed, inasmuch as the audience is uncertain of what their position is in the illusion. The value of this disturbance, however, might rest in the effect it creates of Nazi followers being "blind" and perhaps unthinking, or at least uncritical in their allegiance, not really knowing "which end is up" or "which way to face."

Condition Six: This is a variation of Condition Five, in which a motion picture of Hitler is used. If the characters now face upstage and look, from the same perspective as the audience, at the motion picture of Hitler reviewing the troops, the illusion of being in the same condition as the characters is fuller for the audience than in any of the other conditions discussed so far, because the motion picture seems real.

Condition Seven: This interesting possibility for creating an alienation effect is at once powerful and complex. Although the ramifications of the interpretation are many, let me simply describe the condition itself. The characters, as in Condition One, face the audience and shout and salute as though they were hailing Hitler himself, but the image on the screen upstage is that of a suffering Jew in a concentration camp. In this scene, the music is the *Horst Wessel Lied*, and the characters are patriotically transported in their shouting. Then the music fades as they shout, and the audience begins to hear the plaintive sound of Hebrew music. At this point, the music and the image on the screen correspond, and the effect of sorrow deepens. Without the music of the *Horst Wessel Lied* to support them, the characters' "*Sieg Heils*" grow weaker, and the Hebrew music even begins to contradict them. The characters on stage are now, in effect, drawn into a recognition that something is going on "behind their backs," and they slowly turn around to see what the audience has been looking at all along. Their shouting has now stopped, and their salutes have given place to arms hanging at their sides. Now the audience is no longer at odds with the characters, but in the same position. The major effect of alienation created by Condition Seven is this: When the characters *saw* the concentration camp, they, like the audience, neither shouted nor saluted; is it then not possible that the audience, like the characters, might well have joined the saluters and shouters if they had not seen the camp and had, like the characters, been ignorant of what was going on behind *their* backs?

The examples of how alienation can work to feature the text in Readers Theatre are probably more numerous than there are works of literature to discuss. What should be remembered, however, is the primary value of alienation for Readers Theatre. Carefully used, alienation encourages the audience to think, and it can be an excellent means of providing the audience with critical insights into the text being performed.

Conclusion

Thus far our discussion of staging problems in Readers Theatre has been concerned with single problems in single scenes. Literature, however, is not always so considerate as to supply us with only one problem at a time. Let us, then, conclude this chapter by looking at the following scene from Nelson Algren's "A Bottle of Milk for Mother"—a scene in which the action is rather complicated—and see how we might apply several of the principles discussed so far in staging this scene.

The Lone Wolf of Potomac Street waited miserably, in the long unlovely corridor, for the sergeant to thrust two fingers through the back of his belt. Didn't they realize that he might have Dropkick and Catfoot and Benkowski with a sub-machine gun in a stream-lined cream-colored roadster right down front, that he'd zigzag through the courtroom onto the courtroom fire-escape and—swish—down off the courtroom roof three stories with the chopper still under his arm and through the car's roof and into the driver's seat? Like that George Raft did the time he was innocent at the Chopin, and cops like Adamovitch had better start ducking when Lefty Bicek began making a run for it. He felt the fingers thrust over-familiarly between his shirt and his belt.[24]

The narration in the paragraph preceding the one quoted here tells us that Adamovitch is about five yards behind Bicek, "coming up catfooted like an old man who has been a citizen-dress man can come up catfooted, just far enough behind and just casual enough to make it appear unimportant whether the boy made a run for it or not."[25]

The first sentence of the quoted paragraph refers to two actions one static ("waited") and one dynamic ("thrust"). Between the two references to fingers thrust through the belt, one in the first sentence and one in the last sentence, occurs Bicek's fantasy of escape. There are, then, three phases of the action in this scene:

1. The action of Adamovitch's closing the five yard gap between himself and Bicek to accomplish the thrust of his fingers through Bicek's belt (the *second* reference to this action).

2. The action of Bicek's waiting for the thrust of Adamovitch's fingers through his belt (this is the *anticipated* action, referred to in the first statement about thrusting fingers through the belt).

3. The elaborate action of the fantasy escape by Bicek.

In the realistic or representational theatre, it would be difficult to separate these actions in any way that would emphasize their psychological value, a value that is critical in this particular short story. But Readers Theatre principles may provide a possible means of demonstrating the psychological *and* social values. The focus of the action can be placed out front rather than one stage, in order to control the dissociation of the behavior in the scene. With the actors facing the audience, Adamovitch then moves in slow motion toward the audience and Bicek. Bicek remains frozen like a statue waiting for the finger thrust, his body slightly bent forward as though hanging a little from the waist. The narrator moves in quick pantomime motion to accomplish all the action of the fantasy escape. The speech of the actors can reinforce the three levels of velocity. The first sentence of the paragraph is spoken in very slow speech. But beginning with the second sentence, the speech (which may be assigned to either Bicek or the narrator) increases in rate, matching the increased tempo of the pantomime. The last sentence of the paragraph returns the tempo of speech and action to normal. At this point, the action becomes uncomplicated and realistic, and we might decide to shift the scene back on stage to underscore the contrast between the two scenes.

This suggested staging demonstrates several qualities in the text. First of all, the "ground" for the "figure" of Adamovitch is a medium somewhat denser than air. The impression may be that of a sluggish Juggernaut bearing down inexorably on poor Bicek through this medium; or it may be that of a soft, floating, romantic idyll, which in this situation would create an alienation effect. Bicek's frozen position may suggest that he is trapped and that his situation is inescapable, or it may suggest that he lacks the life force to enter into the romantic image of the floating Adamovitch. The hectic, frantic, helter-skelter gyrations of the narrator as he enacts Bicek's fantasy of escape suggest the anxiety of Bicek. The narrator's actions also contrast the inescapable realities of Bicek's true condition with his unrealistic fantasy life, which has been his weakness all along. The ground for the narrator figure is thinner than air and offers little resistance in the way of gravity. The contrasts in the actions of all three figures lends precision to our interpretation of the scene, which is skillfully realized in the written or spoken text when a fantasy is placed in parenthetic relation between two statements about thrust fingers in a belt—the first, an *anticipated* action, and the second, a *realized* action.

One final point should be made, concerning the reason that the Readers Theatre presentation of this scene is apt to be more successful in featuring the text of Algren's story than a more conventional representational production on stage. In the staging suggested above, the action of Adamovitch is *somewhat* realistic; the action of Bicek is *entirely* realistic; and the action of the narrator is somewhat *un*realistic. Putting the scene out front allows the audience to fill out the details of the scene and the action outlined in the narration, and the narrator's physical pantomime supports the scene with suggested semi-realistic movement. Adamovitch moves very little on stage, and so he does not seriously contradict the imagined quality of the narrator's actions. Bicek is the most realistic in his behavior, but since he moves not at all, or almost not at all, he offers even less contradiction than Adamovitch. It is a beautifully orchestrated scene when staged in the way suggested, for we can easily see the differences and at the same time the relationship between reality and fantasy, which is central to the story.

chapter five
Designing

Designing and selecting costumes, properties, and settings for a Readers Theatre production present rather special problems, because the designer's task is to design in the interest of featuring the text and supporting the director's interpretation of the text. A very beautiful, highly imaginative setting will have no particular value in a Readers Theatre production if it has little or no relation to the text being performed. The same holds true for the absence of any specific set pieces. Neither is valuable in itself for Readers Theatre, except as it may serve to support or feature a particular text.

We might begin by assuming that such aspects of a production as settings, costumes, and properties are always present in theatrical productions, regardless of the style of the performance. Even a bare stage is a kind of setting, that is, a physical environment in which the actors perform. Even rehearsal clothing is a kind of costume, that is, the clothing which the actors wear. The objects used by the characters, whether actual or imagined, are properties. If we grant these assumptions, that the actors must wear something, that they must perform somewhere, and that they must acknowledge the handling of props by the characters in the text, then the designer's job is to make these costumes, settings, and properties functional in featuring the text.

Literal Versus Suggested Costumes, Properties, and Settings

Let us consider, first of all, some of the relative values of literal and suggested costumes, properties, and settings for Readers Theatre. In general, productions that attempt to literalize all costumes, settings, and properties, as well as those that attempt to suggest them, may have decided disadvantages for Readers Theatre. In the first place, both kinds of productions are usually interested in featuring special kinds of performances rather than featuring a particular text. A production in which everything is literalized has the advantage of making the text's experience more realistic, possibly more immediate, and possibly more pleasant to look at; it also runs the risk of obscuring the text in visual effects or imposing realism on a production when realism is not called for by the text. On the other hand, if all costumes, properties, and settings in a text are left to the audience's imagination, the audience's imagination must be carefully controlled so that it is directed toward the experience of the text. The designer in Readers Theatre, then, needs some guidelines to follow in deciding which costumes, properties, and settings to literalize, which to suggest, and how to literalize or suggest them in order to feature the text.

As was pointed out in the preceding chapter, any literary text is composed of generalities and particularities. Sometimes these are in the nature of the language; sometimes they are in the nature of costumes, properties, and settings. We might say, then, that costumes, properties, and settings that are particularized in the text should be particularized in the performance; whatever is generalized in the text should be generalized in the performance. Literalizing costumes, props, and sets, in general, tends to particularize them, whereas suggesting them tends to generalize them. In the latter instance, the audience (like the silent reader) uses its imagination to fill out the details. For example, when Othello instructs Emilia to draw by the curtains, the curtains are generalized; but the handkerchief that he gives to Desdemona is not just any handkerchief. It is quite particularized in the text—several characters recognize it by sight, it is embroidered rather elaborately, and so forth. The actor, then, would be allowed to suggest the curtain (probably through pantomime), but a literal handkerchief, which resembles the one described in the play, would be used. There is another reason for literalizing the handkerchief in a Readers Theatre production of *Othello*, and this is that this particular handkerchief plays an important part in supplying Othello with specific "ocular proof" of Desdemona's alleged infidelity.

A similar observation can be made regarding costumes. Let us consider, for example, Schiller's *Maid of Orleans*, a treatment of the Joan of Arc story à la German Romanticism. Because the soldiers in this play are "generalized soldiers," we might costume them in some sort of generalized military uniform. Schiller makes it quite clear, however, that Joan's military costume is an integral part of the play—particularly her sword, banner, and helmet. If we costume the soldiers in generalized military garb, then we might costume Joan in a more elaborate military outfit, complete with a special sword, helmet, and banner. But we could probably emphasize more clearly the symbolic value of Joan's costume if we dress the soldiers and Joan in some kind of basic costume (tights and tunics, for example, with some suggestion of the military) and also supply Joan with her three important costume pieces. Such stylized costuming has the added virtue of supporting the nonrealistic style of the play.

Designing settings for Readers Theatre may seem somewhat more complex than designing costumes or properties. For instance, when the settings of a text constantly shift from general to particular, the designer has a difficult problem—but not an insurmountable one. The designer of settings for *War and Peace* would have a major task before him if he attempted to literalize every setting. But in the APA-Phoenix's production of Tolstoy's novel, a very imaginative and functional set was designed, which consisted of adjustable platforms, step units, drapes, scrims, and several pieces of furniture. Using a variety of combinations of the unit set and selected set pieces, the designer was able to shift quickly and easily from general settings such as "a Moscow street" to specific settings such as "Prince Andrey's room."

The possibilities inherent in suggested settings can also be seen in terms of movement. As a rule, most settings in conventional theatre are fairly rigid while the actors are mobile. But if we allow the set to move while the actors remain immobile, we may well be able to create various kinds of tensions between characters and their environments, which certain texts may demand. Let us say, for example, that Actor A stands on a low platform, on which a frame is built. Actor B is standing next to the platform. Character A says, "I wish John would come home." Character B says, "I don't want to go home." If the platform is on casters, the frame can be moved to include B. When A then says, "I'm glad you're home," we have the same illusion of former separation and present togetherness that we would have in a literalized setting. But when the house moves to include B, rather than actor B walking across the stage into the house, we also have a more vivid experience of Character B's resistance. The "frame theory" of movement, which was discussed in Chapter Four, can be applied in many other ways in designing settings that will create the special tensions that characterize a particular scene, character, text, and so forth.

Suggested costumes, props, and settings, then, have the virtues of allowing the audience to use its imagination to fill out the details and allowing the visual elements of the production to provide imaginative extensions of the experience beyond the merely literal level. Because many texts rely on the reader's imagination to perform such services, the Readers Theatre director and designer may rely fairly heavily on suggested costumes, props, and settings. However, as was pointed out earlier, they must exercise a good deal of artistic control, so that the suggestions will direct the audience's response toward the experience of the text. It simply is not true that the audience will disregard the visual effects on the stage if the effects have little relevance to the text being performed. The audience will recognize discrepancies that may exist, and this will no doubt interfere with their enjoyment of the full experience of the text. For example, costuming all of the actors in modern corduroy shirts may serve to neutralize the *actors* but it may also suggest something casual about the manner of the *characters*. Such costuming could hardly be appropriate for a text such as Schiller's *Maid of Orleans,* in which the characters and style are anything but casual. Such considerations also apply to the use of suggested props. If the designer were to substitute a butter knife for a dagger, for the purpose of "suggesting" that one character is threatening another character with a lethal weapon, the effect would be ludicrous. This might be valuable if the tone of the scene is humorous but if the audience is supposed to take the threat seriously, such an effect would seriously distort the text. If the Readers Theatre director fails to recognize the social or psychological equivalents of his "suggestions," he may well not understand why the audience expresses a preference for a more "literalized" production. On the other hand, his recognition and application of these equivalents can lead to a more exciting and more insightful experience of the text than a totally literalized production would allow.

Let us look at an example of how suggested settings, props, and costumes that have been carefully and imaginatively selected in terms of the text not only can serve to feature the text, but also can encourage the audience's awareness of the fullness and immediacy of the social and psychological values of the text's experience. This scene and the discussion that follows are based on a chamber theatre production of Dylan Thomas' unfinished novel, *Adventures in the Skin Trade.*[1] In the scene, young Samuel Bennett, newly arrived in London, has been taken to an upstairs bathroom in Mrs. Dacey's shop where Mrs. Dacey's daughter Polly is going to help Sam disengage a bottle that has become stuck on his finger. The bathroom is described as dimly lit, dingy, and filled with birdcages whose inhabitants make loud screeching noises. Sam is seated on the rim of the bathtub, in which a rubber duck floats on the used, greasy water. Much to Samuel's dismay and discomfort, Polly has just suggested that they go for a swim—in the bathtub.

Sam: She wants me to sit with my overcoat on and my bottle on my finger in the cold greasy bath, in the half-dark bathroom, under the sneering birds. I've got on a new suit, Polly.

Polly: Take it off, silly. I don't want you to go in the bath with your clothes on. Look, I'll put something over the window, so you can undress in the dark. Then I'll undress too. I'll come in the bath with you. Sam, are you frightened?

Sam: I don't know. Couldn't we take our clothes off and not go in the bath? I mean, if we want to take them off at all. Someone might come in, it's terribly cold, Polly. Terribly cold.

Polly: You're frightened. You're frightened to lie in the water with me. You won't be cold for long.

Sam: But there's no sense in it. I don't want to go in the bath. Let's sit here and you do being glad, Polly.

Narrator: He could not move his hand, she had caught the bottle between her legs.

Polly: You don't want to be frightened. I'm not any older than you are,

Narrator: She said, and her whispering mouth was close to his ear.

Polly: As soon as you get in the bath I'll jump on top of you in the dark. You can pretend I'm somebody you love if you don't like me properly. You can call me any name.

Sam: She dug her nails into his hand.

Polly: Give me your coat, I'll hang it over the window. Dark as midnight,

Narrator: She said, as she hung the coat up, and her face in the green light through the curtains was like a girl's under the sea. Then all the green went out, and he heard her fumbling.

Sam: I do not want to drown. I do not want to drown in Sewell Street off Circe Street.

Polly: Are you undressing? I can't hear you. Quick, quick, Sam.

Narrator: He took off his jacket and pulled his shirt over his head.

Sam: Take a good look in the dark, Mortimer Street, have a peek at me in London. I'm cold, Polly.

Polly: I'll make you warm, beautifully warm, Sam.

Narrator: He could not tell where she was, but she was moving in the dark and clinking a glass.

Polly: I'm going to give you some brandy. There's brandy, darling, in the medicine cupboard. I'll give you a big glass. You must drink it right down.

Narrator: Naked, he slipped one leg over the edge of the bath and touched the icy water.

Sam: Come and have a look at impotent Samuel Bennett from Mortimer Street off Stanley's Grove trembling to death in a cold bath in the dark near Paddington Station. I'm lost in the metropolis with a rubber duck and a girl I cannot see pouring brandy into a tooth glass. The birds are going mad in the dark. It's been such a short day for them, Polly. I'm in the bath now.

Polly: I'm undressing too. Can you hear me? That's my dress rustling. Now I'm taking my petticoat off. Now I'm naked.

Narrator: A cold hand touched him of the face.

Polly: Here's the brandy, Sam. Sam, my dear, drink it up and then I'll climb in with you. I'll love you, Sam. I'll love you up. Drink it all up and then you can touch me.

Narrator: He felt the glass in his hand and he lifted it up and drank all that was left in it.

Sam: Christ!

Narrator: He said in a clear, ordinary voice.

Sam: Christ!

Narrator: Then the birds flew down and kicked him on the head, carefully between the eyes, brutally on each temple, and he fell back in the bath.[2]

In the production of *Adventures in the Skin Trade* from which this scene was taken, the stage was bare during the bathroom scene, except for a bench placed down center. The bench served as the actual bathtub and as a part of the imagined places where, earlier in the scene, Sam and Polly fancied they were enjoying an outing by the sea. The aesthetic value of the birds and the birdcages was not so much in their visual effect as in their aural effect; consequently, the infernal screeching of the birds was taped, and played from time to time during the scene. The only literal prop used was the bottle attached to Sam's finger, because this rather ludicrous "extension" was particularly important (throughout the novel, Sam never manages to disengage the bottle). It might seem that the glass of brandy is particularized enough in the text to be literalized in the production. But Sam's dilemma at the end of the scene occurs because Polly has inadvertently poured eau de Cologne, rather than brandy, into the tooth glass. It is important in the scene that we *not* know Polly's mistake.

The costumes for the scene included slacks and pullover sweaters for Sam and the narrator, plus a tweed sport jacket for Sam. Polly wore a dress with a full skirt and low-necked bodice. Under these costumes, Polly and Sam wore their suggested "skins," which consisted of long-sleeved leotards and tights—bright blue for Sam and bright red for Polly. The characters' outer costumes seemed to possess the rather informal, tweedy exterior tone of the characters. The leotards and tights, however, seemed to be a particularly imaginative suggestion. If the scene were staged literally, and Polly and Sam were both naked, the emphasis in the scene would no doubt shift from what it was in the text. Putting them in leotards allowed the audience the illusion of nakedness in general, without emphasizing the particulars of their individual nakedness. Furthermore, the blue tights provided a visual counterpart of Sam's exaggerated coldness in an outrageous manner, which paralleled the outrageous tone of this scene. Polly's red outfit made her seem, in her equally unreal "skin," as outrageously hot-blooded to the audience as she does to Sam. Probably the most important aspect of the staging of this scene was the director and designer's awareness of the narrative point of view in the story, which was reflected in the costuming, settings, and props. All of the visual and aural effects served also to direct the audience toward seeing the story through Samuel's attitude and responses, that is, seeing it from his point of view. It is just this kind of careful attention to the text and its visual counterparts that can make Readers Theatre an exciting critical and theatrical experience.

Aesthetic Values of Traditional Features of Readers Theatre

We have previously discussed the aesthetic value of such traditional Readers Theatre features as directing lines out front and minimizing movement. Let us now consider some traditional features of Readers Theatre that are directly related to the subject of this chapter.

In many traditional Readers Theatre productions, the stage is decorated with stools or reading stands. Also, the people on stage usually carry some kind of book or manuscript. I qualify these statements, because there are apparently as many Readers Theatre directors who deviate from these principles as there are purist practitioners. It is also observable that in most conventional theatre productions, the performers do not carry their scripts, and they do not use reading stands. We are not concerned here, however, with prescribing rules for featuring a special kind of performance. Rather, we are interested in exploring the psychological and aesthetic values of such practices in both kinds of theatre, in order to formulate some principles that we can apply in a theatre interested in featuring a literary text.

Let us begin by considering the function of such stage properties as stools, benches, and ladders. Generally speaking, all of these are relatively free of connotation; they are merely articles upon which to sit. Their greatest value for the Readers Theatre director is their flexibility. Furthermore, because they are rather skeletal in their structures, they allow the audience to fill out the details of the setting, according to the demands of the text. As was pointed out earlier, the bench used in the bathroom scene in *Adventures in the Skin Trade* allowed the audience the dual experience of the realistic bathtub and the beaches of Sam's imagination. Another scene in this same production took place in "A Room Full of Furniture."[3] In the production, benches, stools, and step ladders were piled together in a cluttered, abstract arrangement that was skeletal enough to allow the audience some imaginative extension. But the arrangement produced the illusion that the furnishings were bursting out of their environment. The bizarre set, then, managed also to convey some of the bizarre quality of the text, as the actors moved through, around, and over this maze of furniture.

In the production of *Winnie-the-Pooh* that we discussed previously, stools served still another function. At the opening, the children brought out three stools, which were decorated with colored pillows. Three of the children sat on these stools while the storyteller began talking to them about the stories. Then, when the storyteller suggested that they help her "act out the story," the stools were lined up perpendicular to the proscenium and tied together with a rope. They then provided the boundary line that designated the onstage and offstage areas for the stories. On one side of the stools, the actors played children; on the other side, they played animals.

One final consideration should be given to set pieces (stools, platforms, and so on) that elevate the actors. Theatre history shows us that the elevation of a character on stage over the other characters gives the illusion of control. In the theatres of the Greeks, the third tier supported a statue of the god who was, in effect, controlling the fates of the characters. In the medieval traveling troupes, it was not uncommon for the puppeteer to manipulate his characters (that is, control their actions) above the stage and in full view of the audience. This principle could be used in Readers Theatre, however, to indicate any kind of control—the social control of Theseus and Hippolytus in *A Midsummer Night's Dream,* the psychological control of the husband in *Angel Street,* economic control, emotional control, or even "fate" or "destiny." In the production of *War and Peace* referred to earlier, the narrator set up chess pieces to represent the soldiers, bridges, large buildings, and so forth involved in Napoleon's invasion of Russia. He walked around and through these set pieces, knocking over the slain "people" with a pointer. The effect of this staging was far more horrifying than realism could have managed.

Another traditional feature of Readers Theatre is the lectern, reading stand, or music stand, which is used to hold the actor's script. Although the presence of reading stands on stage will no doubt immediately signal the audience that it is about to witness a special kind of performance, what is their value in a theatre that is featuring the text? Unless reading stands are used to feature the particular text in some way, there is not much value in using them. On the other hand, there does seem to be a principle that could be used to great advantage by a Readers Theatre director: The effect of a reading stand or lectern on the audience and the characters without reading stands is one of restriction. This principle was applied in the early fourth wall realistic theatre, where furniture was frequently placed between the audience and the actors in order to cut off the audience from the actors. We can also see this principle at work in Restoration and eighteenth-century drama (and social life), where the fan was used as a social barrier or "restriction." We might apply this principle in a Readers Theatre production in order to suggest many kinds of restrictions. Lecterns could be provided for characters who are restricted in any number of ways. For example, the restriction could be the closed mind of Lear, the physical restriction of The Imaginary Invalid, the psychological restrictions that prevent Hamlet from taking action, the social restrictions Shylock faces as a Jewish money-lender, or the emotional restrictions of Hedda Gabler. The lectern could also symbolize the disguise in such texts as many Elizabethan plays, where the original audience was aware, for example, that Ganymede was indeed the disguised Rosalind in *As You Like it*, that Fidelio was the disguised Imogene in *Cymbeline*, and so forth.

The lectern principle may also work in a reverse manner: The use of a character without a reading stand or lectern, in the midst of characters with lecterns, emphasizes that character's openness or lack of restraint, and makes him seem freer than the other characters. One excellent recognition and application of this principle can be found in the production of *Peter Pan* that was mentioned in Chapter Three. In this production, all of the actors playing Darling children had lecterns; however, when Peter first appeared, he had no reading stand, which tended to emphasize his freedom. Then, when Wendy and the boys joined him to fly to Never Never Land, they left their reading stands behind them. Captain Hook shifted from seeming completely confined behind his lectern to seeming fully free when he left it to cavort around the stage. Such effects certainly seemed to underscore quite well the essential ideas of restraints and lack of restraints (of all kinds) that Barrie's play is interested in juxtaposing.

In addition to stools and lecterns, another traditional feature of Readers Theatre is the manuscript, which is carried or used in some way by the performers. Although there are certainly exceptions to this general practice, most traditional Readers

Theatre directors seem compelled to have the physical manuscript on stage and in the hands of the performers, usually
because they feel that the presence of the manuscript encourages the audience to feel that the performance is a literary
experience. As was pointed out in Chapter One, however, the
physical book does not necessarily equal the experience of the
text. Nonetheless, because the Readers Theatre director's consideration has traditionally been performance-oriented rather
than text-oriented, he frequently finds himself saying, "Since
I'm stuck with having to use the book, what do I do with it?"
Too often, also, a complaint about Readers Theatre productions is: "Why don't the actors get rid of their books if they
know their lines? Or, don't they know their lines?" We would
like to suggest that neither of these questions has much relevance for Readers Theatre as we have described it in this book.
Obviously, if the text is better served by not using scripts, then
the actors should not use them. On the other hand, it is also
possible that the presence of the manuscript in some form can
perform a valuable aesthetic function in featuring the total
experience of the text. We would suggest that the Readers Theatre director ask himself: "Can the presence of a manuscript
or book on stage perform any particular aesthetic function in
this production? If so, then where and how?" Let us explore,
then, some of the ways in which the physical manuscript can
function in terms of the experience of a particular text.

We might begin with a general principle that can be applied
to the use of scripts in any production: The actor using a
script as part of his performance emphasizes the presence of
actor and character simultaneously, rather than character alone
(as in the conventional theatre) or actor alone (as in the case
of a poor performer). The manuscript is functional for the
actor, not the character; yet the character apparently uses the
manuscript. This principle is closely allied to Brecht's alienation effect, Yeats' use of masks in his dance dramas, and the
psychological principle of "letting the auditors in on the feigning."[4] By making the audience aware of the simultaneous yet
distinct presence of actor and character through the use of
the script, the Readers Theatre production can present literary
material for the audience's critical evaluation as well as for

their emotional involvement. The use of the principle might be quite effective in the presentation of material with social commentary, such as Swift's *Irish Tracts* or Ibsen's *An Enemy of the People,* or material that calls for social action, such as some of Lawrence Ferlinghetti's protest poems or James Baldwin's essays on civil rights. The principle, however, applies to the use of any kind of feigning, alienation, or masking that tends to give the audience a "double view."

The alienation effect created by the use of manuscripts may work in a general way; that is, it may simply encourage a double view by the audience of character and actor. In many instances, however, alienation may be achieved through attention to the specific function of a manuscript in a performance of a text. In such cases, the alienation directs the audience's responses toward the particular aspects of the text that are made to stand out, because the director has exerted more control over the audience's appreciation and critical understanding of the particular text being performed. Consequently, the manuscripts are really aesthetically functional in the given performance. Simple black notebooks or paperback editions of the text, for example, certainly create special effects and communicate certain qualities of tone and style which, however, may have no aesthetic relevance to the particular text being performed. Let us consider some examples of aesthetically functional manuscripts in Readers Theatre productions. One example can be found in Flannery O'Connor's "Everything That Rises Must Converge," in which the attitudes of Julian and his mother, throughout most of the story, are fairly fixed. Julian takes a traditional liberal line while his mother's speeches reflect the traditional conservative attitude. Their attitudes and speeches seem to have come from a book. Consequently, in one production of the story, the actors used scripts and read the fixed parts of their dialogue from the scripts. When the characters suddenly face a situation at the end of the story where they must act spontaneously, not out of any predetermined patterns of behavior, the actors dropped their books along with the characters' fixed responses.

In the production of *Winnie-the-Pooh* that was discussed earlier, the manuscripts were used for two purposes: to underscore the desired alienation and to parallel an effect created by Milne in his printed text. On stage was a large toy box, which contained the animal costumes and several editions and bindings of the Pooh stories. While the narrator and the animals went through the stories, the "children" in the offstage area of the stage sometimes listened to the storyteller and sometimes followed the story in one of the books. Alienation was thereby created through the double view of children and animals. The storyteller carried a large storybook, which she referred to by reading from it and pointing out pictures of the animals in it. On other occasions, the storyteller put the book down and talked to the animals and children with seeming spontaneity. Her relationship to the manuscript not only paralleled the alienation operating with the children-animals, but also managed to create much of the double feeling of written and spoken text that characterizes Milne's storytelling style— a style that alternates between comments such as "you read earlier" and "as I've already told you."

In one production of Alain Robbe-Grillet's *Jealousy*, scripts were used in a very interesting way, which served to illuminate a special quality of the text. The narrated lines were assigned to characters designated as "the director," "the designer," "the lighting technician," and "the costumer." In this manner, the performance illuminated the peculiar narrative quality of this novel, which reads more like a scenario complete with technical directions. In the production, the actors playing directional and technical roles carried their scripts on clipboards and improvised from time to time with the other actors. The astonishing effect of this production was to make the audience rather uncertain as to what was being improvised and what was dictated by the script. This is an uncertainty that permeates the tone and style of the novel as well as its point of view.

Let us consider one final illustration of how manuscripts may function in Readers Theater productions. They may demonstrate the difference between the structure (or grammar) of written language and the structure of spoken language. There is much evidence historically of the close relationship between writing and oral reading. The grammar of literary or written texts will control the oral presentation. Readers Theatre can dramatize the special conditions of a spoken literary text in many ways. Let us say that Character A confesses to Character B something that has been on his mind for some time. His expressions have the quality of having been composed internally—that is, they lack immediacy and spontaneity. While he speaks out front to envisioned Character B, the actress playing B is on stage, and she reads conscientiously from her printed text, even turning a page to emphasize her reception of the message from the printed page rather than from an envisioned Character A out front. This divorce of A's oral speech from B's written message is evident; but it is less real than apparent, because A's confession, delivered in the manner of a disposition, is equivalent to the medieval teacher's mode of dictation called *modus pronuntiantium.* The important point involved here is clarified by Marshall McLuhan, as he notes that before the separation of visual and oral reading, "the reader or consumer was literally involved as a producer."[5] In the example given, Character B is an active producer, rather than a passive listener, of A's oral confession, because as her eyes take in the visual stimulus of the printed text, she is apparently producing for herself in a highly imaginative way the oral fidelity of the printed text she is reading. The audience is not reading her text; the audience is hearing her printed text from the mouth of A. In a very real sense, the Readers Theatre presentation of the scene as described has more aesthetic integrity than the illusions of the realistic theatre will allow.

It is quite possible, then, for Readers Theatre productions to use manuscripts in order to achieve a particular effect that serves the text. The Readers Theatre director and designer must be concerned, however, with the aesthetic function of the manuscript in their production, what kind(s) of manuscripts to use, who should use them, and how and when they should be used, in order to clarify, extend, or provide insight into the specific text being performed.

Stage Shapes

Thus far in our discussions of movement, scene placement, scenery design, and other aspects of staging in Readers Theatre, we have been talking about one kind of stage: the proscenium stage. Ideally, however, the Readers Theatre director and designer ought to be able to make such adjustments in the shape of the stage and the relationship of the audience to the stage's action as are demanded by a particular text. I should like to consider briefly now some of the principles of movement and visual perception as they apply to the relative values of various stage shapes in Readers Theatre.

Let us begin with the relationship of perceived motion to a "framed" stage. The most important principle to be considered here concerns what Wassily Kandinsky calls "directed tensions."[6] It has been noted in recent studies that the directed tensions of objects tend to determine the direction of motion perceived in them. These studies of "gamma motions" refer to the appaent motion in objects when they appear and disappear. For example, a circle seems to expand from its center when it appears and to move centripetally when it disappears. A square seems to unfold in the direction of its sides, with the strongest thrust being horizontal, the next strongest being vertical, and the weakest thrust being downward. When we apply these principles to the thrust of action in Readers Theatre, we can see the possibilities of controlling the dynamics of the action according to the needs of the text. Such control could be exercised, for example, through the use of adjustable frames on stage.

Let us say that two characters are framed in an open square frame in the middle of a proscenium stage, which is also a square frame. Character A is seated at the left edge of the frame while Character B paces back and forth between A and the right edge of the square. The moving character is strengthened in his movement, because he is following the line of directed tension that is strongest (horizontal). Character A stands and sits, moving vertically and downward, along the weaker lines of directed tension. Let us say, then, that the moving character, Character B, reaches some moment of triumphant strength, makes a strong assertion of a conservative status quo position, for instance, and stands still in the middle of the frame. Let us also say that Character A then makes a sudden revolutionary response to the status quo position and thrusts his leg and arm horizontally outside the frame to the left. This violent, and for him unexpected, gesture that moves along the line of strongest directed tension (horizontal) now bursts the very frame of the square. Finally, if further intensity of reaction is needed from him, he can move to the left even farther, outside the square frame altogether. At this point the directed tension will be transferred to the square of the proscenium itself, and the character begins to move along the strongest line of directed tension in the larger frame of the proscenium.

There are essentially two principles involved here, which the Readers Theatre director and designer must recognize:

1. "Gamma motion" suggests that the shape of an object has some observable relationship to dynamics of movement along the lines of directed tension.

2. "Perceived locomotion is enhanced when it conforms to the directed tensions within the object."[7]

For Readers Theatre, the application of these principles involves a recognition that the characters-actors are moving along or against the lines of directed tension, according to the desired effect within shaped frames—squares, circles, oblongs, free forms, and so on.

The perception of movement and directed tension is frequently dependent on proportion; that is, in such shapes as rectangles and ovals, "there is directed tension along the greater axis."[8] When we consider the implications of this principle for Readers Theatre, we find that in the conventional proscenium theatre, there is an oval of action with the greater axis running from left to right, parallel to the apron. The directed tension of the action, consequently, does not involve the audience along the axis of greatest dynamic drive. On a "thrust stage," on the other hand, the axis of greatest strength is directed at the audience, thus involving them more readily in the action.

Furthermore, as Arnheim points out, "The incompleteness of a well-structured pattern produces a tension toward closure."[9] If the Readers Theatre use of the oval stage thrust into the audience can keep the end of the oval nearest the audience "open," the audience will find itself making an effort to close the oval and hence enter into the dynamics of action on a subliminal level. Consider Figure 3. The open end of the

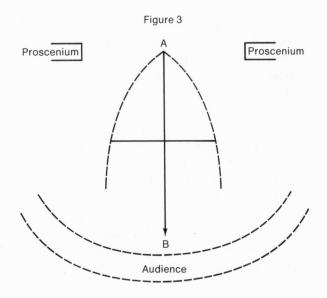

Figure 3

oval at B in Figure 3 is the point of major dramatic tension, where the thrust meets the audience without closure. The audience feels emotionally and psychologically obliged to fill in the responses necessary to close the situation and contain it within the proper confines of the dramatic action. When the audience is arranged in a semicircle, as in Figure 3, the audience members can see each other across and through the action, thus making them aware that they are "outside" the dramatic situation. At the same time, if lines or action are directed toward imagined characters out front, the audience also stands in the position of the characters addressed. Such an arrangement makes an audience somewhat aware of its power—they are not as intrusive as they would be in theatre-in-the-round, nor are they as exclusive as they would be in

conventional proscenium theatre. They are in a dynamic position to effect closure, without the expectation of closure that
is demanded by theatre-in-the-round. The flexibility of directed
tensions allowed by such a stage makes it excellent for literature that is characterized by shifts in the degree and quality
of the audience's involvement.

"Probably the most elementary and effective means of
obtaining directed tension," according to Arnheim, is "oblique
orientation."[10] The importance of obliquity in creating the illusion of movement has already been discussed in Chapter Four.
There is, however, a further significance to this principle as
it applies to the shape of the stage and the stage picture. As
was pointed out, the angle of character relationships on a
proscenium stage tends to be fairly static; the angle of character relationships can appear somewhat more dynamic when
the characters are imagined across an "X" angle out front; the
most dynamic position displays more obliquity than either
conventional theatre or traditional Readers Theatre. Recognition of the principle of obliquity provides the designer with a
means of shifting the angles of character relationships. He may
accomplish this by shifting the size and shape of the area in
which the characters relate, in order to take advantage of the
full range of possible relationships that may exist in a given text.

It is hoped that if the Readers Theatre designer can put to
use some of the compositional skills and principles of the
painter, such as the principle of directed tension, Readers
Theatre can achieve a sense of action that will serve the text
more economically and therefore more effectively than is possible in the conventional theatre.

Lighting

No discussion of visual effects in the theatre would be complete without a consideration of lighting. The Readers Theatre
director will no doubt find that carefully designed lighting can
achieve many effects needed for a particular text. The limitations of this study prohibit our exploring fully the technical
details of lighting design and effects here.[11] Our discussion of

lighting shall be confined to two considerations that affect the Readers Theatre director specifically.

Our earlier discussion of the "general" and the "particular" in a text has relevance for lighting effects, as well as scene placement, costuming, and so forth. The lighting in a text may be general, such as a general mood, a general time of day, a general place; or the lighting may be particular, such as a train's headlight beam, a bolt of lightning, or a flickering light that indicates Tinker Bell in *Peter Pan*. The Readers Theatre director and designer would do well to consider these principles of general and particular when designing the lighting for a production. In one scene of Lawrence Durrell's *An Irish Faustus*, for example, the lighting effects can be particularly important in underscoring the emotional tone of the scene and in paralleling the climax of the scene. The mood is general at the scene's opening, but at the end of the scene we witness the opening of the lower depths and Faustus' triumph over Mephisto. If the quality, degree of intensity and particularity, and timing of the shift in lighting parallels the emotional shift in the characters, the total impact of the scene can be preserved fully and economically.

The final consideration in this chapter concerns the proportionate amount of lighting on stage and in the auditorium. Returning to the history of theatre practice, we can see that through the centuries the decreasing amount of lighting in the auditorium has paralleled a decreased participation by the audience in the experience of the text. In the Greek theatre, in which plays were presented outdoors in the daylight, there was the same lighting for the audience and the actors, and drama was close to a religious ritual and community experience. The drama of the seventeenth- and eighteenth-century theatres in England and France, where plays were performed indoors by candlelight, is marked by an increased separation of audience and characters. Nonetheless, through the use of asides, confidants, and so forth, there was still some interaction. Throughout the nineteenth century, interaction between audience and characters continued to decrease; by the time theatre evolved to the twentieth-century fourth wall theatre, all rapport between audience and characters had disappeared. The

Readers Theatre principle abstracted from this aspect of theatre history, then, is: The more lighting there is in the auditorium, the more the audience is encouraged to participate actively in the experience of the text. It would seem to be necessary, for example, to light the auditorium rather fully in a production of a short story with a very self-conscious narrator, because such 'a narrator is by definition one who is interested in and aware of the audience's responses. Such a principle allows us to shift the degree of lighting in the auditorium as the required audience participation shifts from more to less.

Lighting that is based on this historically abstracted principal may also encourage alienation, but in a rather different way than that discussed earlier. In an auditorium in which the members of the audience are made to feel like participants in the action—not just emotionally moved observers and not just observers in a purely critical position—they are able, by being placed *within* the experience, to get a "deeper inside view." Such was the apparent effect in the 1963 Off Broadway production of Kenneth Brown's play *The Brig*, in which the audience members were made to feel as if they, as well as the characters, were spending "A Night in the Brig."[12] Such effects, which are similar to the "running jumps" described by Robert Bolt in his Preface to *A Man For All Seasons*,[13] depend rather fully on the designer and director's careful attention to the relative amount of lighting on the stage and in the audience.

chapter six

Performing

From time to time in the preceding chapters we have spoken of "aesthetic integrity," a conditon that the contemporary theatre finds hard to achieve or maintain. Among the reasons for this situation is the absence of any clear "decorum" for the actor. If we are to believe the historians, the Elizabethan actor was trained in the decorum of the orator; the laws of rhetoric were fairly clear at that time. Furthermore, the Elizabethan theatre was fundamentally literary; the laws of literature, controlled as they were by rhetorical decorum, were less amorphous than the conglomeration of dialects in our contemporary theatre. Because Readers Theatre is fundamentally a literary theatre, it seems to be in an excellent position to develop and establish some kind of decorum for the actor and the director. To this end, let us consider some basic aspects of the relationship between the performer and the text.

Throughout the discussions of movement and visual effects in Chapters Four and Five, the human actor was generally regarded as an object; indeed human behavior is often mechanical in its effect—so much so that Henri Bergson says that whatever strikes us as comical is the discovery of a mechanical aspect of human behavior. On the other hand, inanimate objects often seem uncannily alive.[1] Readers Theatre can take advantage of this interaction between the mechanical aspect of human behavior and the lively impression often given by inanimate objects in several ways. One way would be to select physical props in terms of their animate value. On the other hand, the manner of the actors' handling of props can increase or decrease the objects' expressive character. Although some objects in literature have value and importance simply because of their presence or existence, the major significance of most objects in literature lies in their relationship to the characters who handle them, observe them, react to them, and so forth. Winnie-the-Pooh's honey pot, for example, is not as important in itself as it is significantly expressive of Pooh. The actor portraying Pooh will need to realize that the honey pot is not simply an object, and that his use of the prop, whether literal or imagined, will have to express the character of Pooh. In the same group of stories by A. A. Milne, Piglet's responses to his balloon are significantly different when the balloon changes from a large red bubble to a "piece of damp rag." And Eeyore's responses to the balloon are decidedly different from Piglet's. Consequently, the manner of handling the props would have to be directed toward expressing the particular character's attitude toward the object.

Similar observations can be made regarding the actor's relationship to his costume. Costumes are actually extensions of one's skin, of oneself. It would be well for the actor to remember this, because his character's costume is not simply clothing for the actor. It has expressive value for the character. If the designer has seen to it that the costume is expressive of the character, the actor must also relate to the costume in such a way that it seems to express *his* character. A casual, relaxed, confident character, for example, costumed in casual attire, will not appear so if the actor seems tense and self-conscious toward his costume. On the other hand, if the characters in and style of the literature are formal, and an actor handles his costume and props "naturally" (that is, in the actor's habitual manner), the text is likely to be quickly distorted. The actor in Readers Theatre, then, must be aware at all times of the expressive value of the costumes and properties—what they express about his character and how they express this. If the character removes a heavy coat, for example, how does he divest himself of the coat? hastily? with grace? wearily? sloppily? What does each manner express? Does the literary style exhibit a certain woodenness or a special kind of grace? How can the actor's use of his body and the extensions of his body (costumes, props, and so forth) express the style?

What an actor is inside is of no consequence in Readers Theatre if to the eye he appears light as a dragonfly, swift as Mercury, or strong as Hercules. He has no more or no less soul than a painted figure in a picture. However, much of the actor's expressiveness comes from the audience's appreciations of deviations from the normal in his behavior. His postures in the character he is expressing will derive strong dynamic properties from the fact that we perceive the poses as deviations from the normal or key position. Furthermore, if alienation is featured, so that the audience is consciously aware of the simultaneous presence of actor and character, a pattern of physical behavior for the *actor* will be established in the performance; this will allow any deviation from this pattern to be expressed more readily and more economically when the actor must express the behavior of his character. On the simplest level, for instance, if the actor moves with a long stride, he can express the mincing quality of his character by taking shorter steps. Such dual behavior also allows the special quality of the character's movement to stand out as clearly his in a way that the contemporary representational theatre does not.

The performer, through his actions, especially in traditional Readers Theatre, is often thought to appeal to the senses of vision and hearing; however, for the actor himself, action is created mostly in the kinesthetic sensations of his muscles, tendons, and joints. If all visual shape is dynamic, as was suggested in Chapter Four, then so too is kinesthetic shape. According to Michotte, "posture is probably experienced as a terminal phase of motion."[2] Merleau-Ponty further points out that "my body appears to me as a posture." When he leans his hands on his desk, the accent is on his hands. The rest of his body trails "like the tail of a comet. . . . My entire posture is, as it were, readable through their [hands] leaning on the desk."[3]

The actor is actually involved with two tensive media—the kinesthetic and the visual. When he lifts his hand, he primarily experiences the tension of raising it. Here the kinesthetic medium communicates the tension to the actor. A similar tension is also visually conveyed to the spectator through the image of the actor's raised arm. In this instance, the medium which communicates the tension is visual. The actor has the responsibility of coordinating these two media for communicating tensions—the visual medium and the kinesthetic medium—into a satisfactory expression of the dramatic moment. With this in mind, we can see that Readers Theatre, with its flexible placement of the scene on stage and out front, allows the actor a flexible environment or "ground" in the staged and/or imagined scene, whereby he can control the audience's responses more forcefully. Consequently, it seems that Readers Theatre can provide the actor with an easier means for coordinating the kinesthetic and visual media than is usual in conventional theatre or traditional Readers Theatre. The kinesthetic medium is "amoebic" in that it has no ground from which it can detach itself as "figure." The actor can judge the size and shape and strength of his motions, but he has little concept of their impact on the visual surrounding field. He must learn how large and fast a gesture should be in order to achieve a desired effect. When the actor has not only gesture, but also speech, there is further need for adjusting his action in the dynamic relationship of figure to ground.

The limitations of the physical body of the actor have made it necessary for the performing arts to remain halfway between the raw material of nature and the precision of controlled form. Conventional theatre has made much of the raw material of nature; as a result, drama has suffered from a rather pedestrian realism. It does seem, however, that Readers Theatre offers the possibility for the development of such "precision of controlled form," so that dramatic literature can be restored to something like the poetic character of Elizabethan drama. If Readers Theatre, like the Elizabethan theatre, is a literary theatre in which the text is being featured, the performers will have to be so skilled in their performances that their performances exist in order to present and feature the text. Such a responsibility is rather different from that imposed by the conventional theatre, wherein the text exists in order to be performed. Yet in spite of the current emphasis on the performance in conventional theatre, it is interesting to note that the performer in Readers Theatre is in an active rather than a passive relationship to the text.

chapter seven

Relating the Text to the Performance

This book has attempted to discover and explore principles for Readers Theatre that would serve to feature the text in a theatrical performance. For the sake of clarity, the illustrations of these principles have been limited to isolated passages of a text. We have not had the benefit of seeing how these principles would operate in the larger context of a production, or how some of the principles discussed in the various chapters might supplement, complement, or even contradict each other. Nonetheless, the Readers Theatre director *will* be faced with such problems in a complete production. Therefore, let us conclude this study by taking a look at a complete Readers Theatre script and suggesting some of the ways in which the principles discussed in this book could be used to clarify, illuminate, extend, or provide insights into the literature being performed.

The following Readers Theatre script was prepared as a composite view of Lawrence Durrell, and was entitled, "Cities, Plains, and People." The script's title, indicative of Durrell's major interests, was taken from one of his volumes of poetry.

The Script

"Bitter Lemons"

In an island of bitter lemons
Where the moon's cool fevers burn
From the dark globes of the fruit,

And the dry grass underfoot
Tortures memory and revises
Habits half a lifetime dead

Better leave the rest unsaid,
Beauty, darkness, vehemence
Let the old sea-nurses keep

Their memorials of sleep
And the Greek sea's curly head
Keep its calms like tears unshed

Keep its calms like tears unshed.[1]

"Lawrence Durrell is the Gauguin of modern poetry, a Gauguin whose Marquesas was an isle of Greece."[2] Thus writes Derek Stanford in an essay on poetic freedom. Writes Durrell, "My skill is in words only." This modesty tells no more than half the truth, for Lawrence Durrell is a poet in the classical sense of the word. And, whether he chooses to cast his writing in lyric verse, travel books, novels, ballads, or plays, the result is inevitably poetry.

Durrell was born in India in 1912 of Anglo-Irish parents. As he writes to his friend Henry Miller about his biography:

Dear H. M.

I was born 27th of February, 1912, at one o'clock of the morning. The Indian blood must have been a mistake. I'm Irish mother, English father. God-fearing, lusty, chapel-going Mutiny stock. My grandma sat up on the verandah of her house with a shotgun across her knee waiting for the Mutiny gang; but when they saw her face they went another way. Hence the family face. I may have a touch of Indian in me, who knows? I'm one of the world's expatriates anyhow. It's lonely being cut off from one's race. So much of England I loved and hated so much. The language clings. I try and wipe it off my tongue but it clings. O what the hell, I was born to be Hamlet's little godchild. The horoscopes can't touch me, I'm already mad![3]

Yours sincerely,
Larry Durrell

"Cities, Plains, and People"

I

Once in idleness was my beginning,

Night was to the mortal boy
Innocent of surface like a new mind
Upon whose edges once he walked
In idleness, in perfect idleness.

O world of little mirrors in the light.
The sun's rough wick for everybody's day;
Saw the Himalayas like lambs there
Stir their huge joints and lay
Against his innocent thigh a stony thigh.

Combs of wind drew through this grass
To bushes and pure lakes
On this tasteless wind
Went leopards, feathers fell or flew:
Yet all went north with the prayer-wheel,
By the road, the quotation of nightingales.

Quick of sympathy with springs
Where the stone gushed water
Women made their water like thieves.

Caravans paused here to drink Tibet.
On draughty corridors to Lhasa
Was my first school
In faces lifted from saddles to the snows:
Words caught by the soft klaxons crying
Down to the plains and settled cities.

So once in idleness was my beginning.
Little known of better then or worse
But in the lens of this great patience
Sex was small,
Death was small,
Were qualities held in a deathless essence,
Yet subjects of the wheel, burned clear
And immortal to my seventh year.

To all who turn and start descending
The long sad river of their growth:
The tidebound, tepid, causeless
Continuum of terrors of the spirit,
I give you here unending
In idleness an innocent beginning

Until your pain become a literature.[4]

Durrell left India at an early age to attend school in England. But his dissatisfaction with the barrenness of England sent him to the islands of the Mediterranean and the Eastern Levant, where the exoticism of the landscape and the people provided him with much of the subject matter for his writing. His book *Bitter Lemons* is an account of the years he spent in Cyprus, and the opening of the book shows Durrell about to embark.

[Note: The designations "Durrell 1" and "Durrell 2" do not appear in Durrell's manuscript. Rather, they refer to the readers who would take these lines in a production.]

Durrell 1: Journeys, like artists, are born and not made. A thousand differing circumstances contribute to them, few of them willed or determined by the will—whatever we may think. They flower spontaneously out of the demands of our natures —and the best of them lead us not only outwards in space, but inwards as well. Travel can be one of the most rewarding forms of introspection.

Durrell 2: These thoughts belong to Venice at dawn, seen from the deck of the ship which is to carry me down through the islands to Cyprus; a Venice wobbling in a thousand fresh-water reflections, cool as a jelly. It was as if some great master, stricken by dementia, had burst his whole colour-box against the sky to deafen the inner eye of the world. Cloud and water mixed into each other, dripping with colours, merging, overlapping, liquefying, with steeples and balconies and roofs floating in space, like the fragments of some stained-glass window seen through a dozen veils of rice-paper. Fragments of history touched with the colours of wine, tar, ocre, blood, fire-opal and ripening grain. The whole at the same time being rinsed softly back at the edges into a dawn sky as softly as circumspectly blue as a pigeon's egg.

Durrell 1: Mentally I held it all, softly as an abstract painting, cradling it in my thoughts—the whole encampment of cathedrals and palaces, against the sharply focused face of Stendhal as he sits forever upon a stiff-backed chair at Florian's sipping wine: or on that of a Corvo, flitting like some huge fruit-bat down these light-bewitched alleys. . . .

Durrell 2: The pigeons swarm the belfries. I can hear their wings across the water like the beating of fans in a great summer ballroom. The *vaporetto* on the Grand Canal beats too, softly as a human pulse, faltering and renewing itself after every hesitation which marks a landing stage. The glass palaces of the Doges are being pounded in a crystal mortar, strained through a prism. Venice will never be far from me in Cyprus—for the lion of Saint Mark still rides the humid airs of Famagusta, of Kyrenia.

It is an appropriate point of departure for the traveller to the Eastern Levant. . . .

Durrell 1: But heavens, it was cold. Down on the grey flagged quay I had noticed a coffee-stall which sold glasses of warm milk and *croissants*. It was immediately opposite the gang plank, so that I was in no danger of losing my ship. A small dark man with a birdy eye served me wordlessly, yawning in my face, so that in sympathy I was forced to yawn too. I gave him the last of my liras.

There were no seats, but I made myself comfortable on an up-ended barrel and, breaking my bread into the hot milk, fell into a sleepy contemplation of Venice from this unfamiliar angle of vision across the outer harbour.

Durrell 2: A tug sighed and spouted a milky jet upon the nearest cloud. The cabin steward joined me for a glass of milk.

Durrell 1: He was an agreeable man, rotund and sleek, with a costly set of dimples round his smile—like expensive cuff-links in a well-laundered shirt.

Steward: Beautiful, he agreed, looking at Venice, beautiful:

Durrell 1: But it was a reluctant admission, for he was from Bologna, and it was hard to let the side down by admiring a foreign city. He plunged into a pipe full of scented shag.

Steward: You are going to Cyprus? he said at last,

Durrell 1: Politely, but with the faintest hint of commiseration.

Durrell 2: Yes. To Cyprus.

Steward: To work?

Durrell 2: To work. It seemed immodest to add that I was intending to live in Cyprus, to buy a house if possible. . . .

Durrell 1: After five years of Serbia I had begun to doubt whether, in wanting to live in the Mediterranean at all, I was not guilty of some fearful aberration;

Durrell 2: Indeed, the whole of this adventure had begun to smell of improbability. I was glad that I was touching wood.

Steward: It is not much of a place, he said.

Durrell 2: So I believe.

Steward: Arid and without water. The people drink to excess.

Durrell 2: This sounded rather better.

Durrell 1: I have always been prepared, where water was scarce, to wash in wine if necessary.

Durrell 2: How is the wine? I asked.

Steward: Heavy and sweet.

Durrell 2: That was not so good. A Bolognese is always worth listening to on the subject of wine.

Durrell 1: No matter (I should buy a small peasant house and settle in the island for four or five years.) The most arid and waterless of islands would be a rest after the heartless dusty Serbian plains.

Steward: But why not Athens?

Durrell 1: He said softly, echoing my own thoughts.

Durrell 2: Money restrictions.

Steward: Ah! Then you are going to live in Cyprus for some time?

Durrell 2: My secret was out.

Durrell 1: His manner changed, and his picture of Cyprus changed with it, for politeness does not permit an Italian to decry another's plans, or run down his native country.

Durrell 2: Cyprus was to become mine by adoption—therefore he must try to see it through my eyes.

Steward: At once it became fertile, full of goddesses and mineral springs; ancient castles and monasteries; fruit and grain and verdant grasslands; priests and gipsies and brigands. . . . *(He continues throughout Durrell's next speech.)*

Durrell 1: He gave a swift Sicilian travel-poster varnish, beaming at me approvingly as he did so.

Durrell 2: And the girls? I said at last.

Durrell 1: But here he stuck; politeness battled with male pride for a long moment.

Durrell 2: He would have to tell the truth lest later on, in the field, so to speak, I might convict him—a Bolognese, above all!—of having no standards of female beauty.

Steward: Very ugly, he said at last, in genuine regret. Very ugly indeed.

Durrell 2: This was disheartening.

Durrell 1: We sat there in silence for a while until the steamer towering above us gave a loud lisp of steam ffffff, while beaded bubbles of condensing steam trickled down the siren.
Durrell 2: It was time to say good-bye to Europe.[5]

• • •

Somewhere between Calabria and Corfu the blue really begins. All the way across Italy you find yourself moving through a landscape severely domesticated—each valley laid out after the architect's pattern, brilliantly lighted, human. But once you strike out from the flat and desolate Calabrian mainland towards the sea, you are aware of a change in the heart of things: aware of the horizon beginning to stain at the rim of the world: aware of *islands* coming out of the darkness to meet you.

In the morning you wake to the taste of snow on the air, and climbing the companion ladder, suddenly enter the penumbra of shadow cast by the Albanian mountains—each wearing its cracked crown of snow—desolate and repudiating stone.

A peninsula nipped off while red hot and allowed to cool into an antarctica of lava. You are aware not so much of a landscape coming to meet you invisibly over those blue miles of water as of a climate. You enter Greece as one might enter a dark crystal; the form of things becomes irregular, refracted. Mirages suddenly swallow islands, and wherever you look the trembling curtain of the atmosphere deceives.

Other countries may offer you discoveries in manners or lore or landscape; Greece offers you something harder—the discovery of yourself.[6]

• • •

"Exile in Athens"

To be a king of islands,
Share a boundary with eagles,
Be a subject of sails.

Here, on these white rocks,
In cold palaces all winter,
Under the salt blanket,

Forget not the tried intent,
Pale hands before the face: face
Before the sea's blue negative,

Washing against the night,
Pushing against the doors,
Earth's dark metaphors.

Here alone in a stone city
I sing the rock, the sea-squill
Over Greece the one punctual star.

To be king of the clock—
I know, I know—to share
Boundaries with the bird,

With the ant her lodge:
But they betray, betray.
To be the owner of stones,

To be a king of islands,
Share a bed with a star,
Be a subject of sails.[7]

• • •

Durrell's romantic escape to the islands of Greece and the Eastern Levant turned out to be more Byronic, however, than he imagined it would be. In November of 1940 he writes to Henry Miller:

Dear Henry:

I hope you will get this some day. At the moment everything is upside down and what with the air raids and one thing and another I hardly have time to think. We are submerged in the struggle. Well, the Epirotes have been having a picnic up there as I promised. Katsimbalis has ridden off gigantically with the artillery; Tonio is away with the fleet—just had a note from George Seferis. In the meantime I have been trying to go up to Corfu with the Navy or Air Force with no result. They say they are not operating at all in the sectors which I want to help with; and the Greeks seem not to need help now. Everyone has been in raptures over Greek successes. Meanwhile the air raid siren has entered our lives three or four times a day: a most unpleasant experience. However, we live and learn. We are in good fettle and so grateful to you for helping us out. My mother is sending you back the dough slowly from London.

I see no end to the business. It will go on for years because we are no nearer to the individual solution—and the outer struggle is only a reflection of it. Nothing remains really except one's personal honour and one's love for the killers. We shall see.

Love to anyone over there who might be in need of disinterested love. Ah Lao-tse, we need you here!

Larry[8]

• • •

It was not long, however, before Durrell joined the British Information Office in Alexandria, Egypt, where he worked almost until the end of the war. It was here that the seeds for his highly acclaimed tetralogy of novels, *The Alexandria Quartet*, were first germinated.

Dear Henry:

Yes, I got the letters. I'm in touch with the embassy, representing them, so they pass them on. Your news sounds marvellous. Of course anything is less than what the world owes you for opening up the world with your own bright eye. Seventeen books sounds an awful lot to me. Let me have any old duplicate proofs that come your way—I haven't read anything of yours since the marvellous Greek book. Here we are sweltering in an atmosphere that demands a toast—great passions, short lives. Everything is worn thin as a eggshell; it's the fifth year now and the nervous breakdown is coming into the open. Old women, ginger dons, nursing sisters begin to behave like bacchantes; they are moving in and out of nursing homes with a steady impetus. Meanwhile we are crippled here by an anemia and an apathy and a censorship which prevents the least trace of the human voice—of any calibre. We exist on a machine-made diet of gun bomb and tank—backed up by the slogan.

The atmosphere in this delta is crackling like a Leyden jar. You see, in normal times all the local inhabitants spend six months in Europe a year, so they are as stale and beaten thin as the poor white collar man. The poetry I exude these days is dark grey and streaky, like bad bacon. But the atmosphere of sex and death is staggering in its intensity. Meanwhile the big shots come and go, seeing nothing, feeling nothing, in a money daydream; there is still butter and whiskey and cafe viennois. A kind of diseased fat spreads over the faces and buttocks of the local populations, who have skimmed the grease off the war effort in contracts and profiteering. No, I don't think you would like it. First this steaming humid flatness—not a mount or hill anywhere—choked to bursting point with bones and the crummy deposits of wiped out cultures. Then this smashed up broken down shabby Neapolitan town, with its Levantine mounds of houses peeling in the sun. A sea flat, dirty brown and waveless rubbing the port. Arabic, Coptic, Greek, Levant French; no music, no art, no real gaiety. A saturated middle European boredom laced with drink and Packards and beach-cabins. NO SUBJECT OF CONVERSATION EXCEPT MONEY. Even love is thought of in money terms. "You are getting on with her? She has ten thousand a year of her own." Six hundred greaseball millionaires sweating in their tarbushes and waiting for the next shot of root-hashish. And the shrieking personal unhappiness and loneliness showing in every face. No, if one could write a single line of anything that had a human smell to it here, one would be a genius.[9]

•   •   •

"Alexandria"

To the lucky now who have lovers or friends,
Who move to their sweet undiscovered ends,

Or whom the great conspiracy deceives,
I wish these whirling autumn leaves:
Promontories splashed by the salty sea,
Groaned on in darkness by the tram
To horizons of love or good luck or more love—
As for me I now move
Through many negatives to what I am.

Here at the last cold Pharos between Greece
And all I love, the lights confide
A deeper darkness to the rubbing tide;
Doors shut, and we the living are locked inside
Between the shadows and the thoughts of peace:
And so in furnished rooms revise
The index of our lovers and our friends
From gestures possibly forgotten, but the ends
Of longings like unconnected nerves,
And in this quiet rehearsal of their acts
We dream of them and cherish them as Facts.

Now when the sea grows restless as a conscript,
Excited by fresh wind, climbs the sea-wall,
I walk by it and think about you all:
B. with his respect for the Object, and D.
Searching in sex like a great pantry for jars
Marked "Plum and apple"; and the small, fel
Figure of Dorian ringing like a muffin-bell—
All indeed whom war or time threw up
On this littoral and tides could not move
Were objects for my study and my love.

And then turning where the last pale
Lighthouse, like a Samson blinded, stands
And turns its huge charred orbit on the sands
I think of you—indeed mostly of you,
In whom the writer would only name and lose
The dented boy's lip and the close
Archer's shoulders; but here to rediscover
By tides and faults of weather, by the rain
Which washes everything, the critic and the lover.

At the doors of Africa so many towns founded
Upon a parting could become Alexandria, like
The wife of Lot—a metaphor for tears;
And the queer student in his poky hot
Tenth floor room above the harbour hears
The sirens shaking the tree of his heart,
And shuts his books, while the most

Inexpressible longings like wounds unstitched
Stir in him some girl's unquiet ghost.

So we, learning to suffer and not condemn
Can only wish you this great pure wind
Condemned by Greece, and turning like a helm
Inland where it smokes the fires of men,
Spins weathercocks on farms or catches
The lovers at their quarrel in the sheets;
Or like a walker in the darkness might,
Knocks and disturbs the artist at his papers,
Up there alone, upon the alps of night.[10]

• • •

Even away from Egypt, the image of Alexandria and its inhabitants never left Durrell. In the summer of 1956 he writes to Henry Miller that he has just finished writing a novel about Alexandria, entitled *Justine*. Indeed, the narrator of this first volume of *The Alexandria Quartet* expresses many of Durrell's own attitudes toward the city and its inhabitants.

The sea is high again today, with a thrilling flush of wind. In the midst of winter you can feel the inventions of spring. A sky of hot nude pearl until midday, crickets in sheltered places, and now the wind unpacking the great planes, ransacking the great planes. . . .

I have escaped to this island with a few books and the child—Melissa's child. I do not know why I use the word "escape." The villagers say jokingly that only a sick man would choose such a remote place to rebuild. Well, then, I have come here to heal myself, if you like to put it that way. . . .

At night, when the wind roars and the child sleeps quietly in its wooden cot by the echoing chimney-piece I light a lamp and walk about, thinking about my friends—of Justine and Nessim, of Melissa and Balthazar. I return link by link down the iron chain of memory to the city which we inhabited so briefly together: the city which used us as its flora—precipitated in us conflicts which were hers and which we mistook for our own: beloved Alexandria!

I have had to come so far away from it in order to understand it all! Living on this bare promontory, snatched every night from darkness by Arcturus, far from the lime-laden dust of those summer afternoons, I see at last that none of us is properly to be judged for what happened in the past. It is the city which should be judged though we, its children, must pay the price.[11]

• • •

The narrator's efforts "to understand it all" manifest themselves as the novel *Justine*. But in *Balthazar*, the second volume of *The*

Alexandria Quartet, we learn, as he does, that much of what he envisioned as "real" was but an illusion:

"We live," writes Pursewarden somewhere, "lives based upon selected fictions. Our view of reality is conditioned by our position in space and time—not by our personalities as we like to think. Thus every interpretation of reality is based upon a unique position. Two paces east or west and the whole picture is changed." Something of this order. . . .

As for human characters, whether real or invented, there are no such animals. Each psyche is really an ant-hill of opposing predispositions. Personality as something with fixed attributes is an illusion—but a necessary illusion *if we are to love!* [12]

• • •

Throughout *The Alexandria Quartet,* many of Durrell's people come face to face with this question of illusion and reality. In *Mountolive,* the third volume of the tetralogy, the confrontation is revealed rather dramatically, in the title character's rendezvous with his former lover. When young David Mountolive had first come to Egypt in the British Diplomatic Service, he had been a lover to Leila Hosnani, the beautiful Coptic mother of his friend Nessim. However, David's diplomatic responsibilities subsequently call him to the continent. He returns to Alexandria twelve years later and the once-beautiful Leila, who now goes veiled to hide the ravages of smallpox, has finally consented to see him. They agree to rendezvous at the park near the Auberge:

[Note: The designations "Narrator," "Mountolive," and "Leila" do not appear in Durrell's manuscript. They are used here to suggest how the lines might be assigned in a chamber theatre adaptation. Italicized lines represent stage directions for the actors.]

Narrator: He crossed the gravel with a light and joyous step, hearing it squeak under his shoes, and as he neared the gharry called, in a soft voice:

Mountolive: Leila! He saw the silhouette of the driver turn against the sky and register attention; from inside the cab he heard a voice—

Narrator: Leila's voice—

Mountolive: Say something like:

Leila: Ah, David, so at last we meet. I have come all this way to tell you . . . *(She continues to improvise until her next speech.)*

Narrator: He leaned forward with a puzzled air, straining his eyes, but could not see more than the vague shape of someone in the far corner of the cab.

Leila: Get in! She cried imperiously. Get in and we shall talk. *(Her improvisation continues.)*

Narrator: It was here that a sense of unreality overtook Mountolive; he could not exactly fathom why.

Mountolive: But he felt as one does in dreams when one walks without touching the ground, or else appears to rise deliberately through the air like a cork through water. His feelings, like antennae, were reaching out towards the dark figure, trying to gather and assess the meaning of these tumbling phrases and to analyse the queer sense of disorientation which they carried, buried in them, like a foreign intonation creeping into familiar voices; somewhere the whole context of his impressions foundered.

Narrator: The thing was this: he did not quite recognize the voice.

Mountolive: Or else, to put it another way, he could identify Leila, but not quite believe in the evidence of his own ears.

Narrator: It was, so to speak, not the precious voice which, in his imagination, had lived on, inhabiting the remembered figure of Leila.

Mountolive: She spoke now with a sort of gobbling inconsistency, an air of indiscretion, in a voice which had a slightly clipped edge on it.

Narrator: He supposed this to be the effect of excitement and who knows what other emotions?

Mountolive: But . . . phrases which petered out, only to start again in the middle, phrases which lapsed and subsided in the very act of joining two thoughts? He frowned to himself in the darkness as he tried to analyse this curious unreal quality of distraction in the voice. It was not the voice that belonged to Leila.

Narrator: Or was it? Presently a hand fell upon his arm and he was able to study it eagerly in the puddle of soft light cast by the oil lamp in the brass holder by the cabby's box. It was a chubby and unkempt little hand, with short, unpainted fingernails and unpressed cuticles.

Mountolive: Leila, is it really you? He asked almost involuntarily, still invaded by this sense of unreality, of disorientation; as of two dreams overlapping, displacing one another.

Leila: Get in.

Narrator: Said the new voice of an invisible Leila.

Mountolive: As he obeyed and stepped forward into the swaying cab he smelt her strange confusion of scents on the night air—

Narrator: Again a troubling departure from the accepted memory. But orange-water, mint, Eau de Cologne, and sesame;

Mountolive: She smelt like some old Arab lady!

Narrator: And then he caught the dull taint of whisky.

Mountolive: She too had had to string her nerves for the meeting with alcohol! Sympathy and indecision battled within him; the old image of the brilliant, resourceful and elegant Leila refused somewhere to fix itself in the new. He simply must see her face.

Leila: As if she read his thoughts, she said, "So I came at last, *unveiled,* to meet you."

Mountolive: He suddenly thought, bringing himself up with a start, "My God! I simply haven't stopped to think how old Leila might be!"

Narrator: She made a small sign and the old jarvey in the tarbush drew his nag slowly back on to the lighted macadam of the Grande Corniche and set the gharry moving at walking pace. Here the sharp blue street-lamps came up one after the other to peer into the cab, and with the first of these intrusive gleams of light Mountolive turned to gaze at the woman beside him.

Mountolive: He could very dimly recognize her. He saw a plump and square-faced Egyptian lady of uncertain years, with a severely pock-marked face and eyes drawn grotesquely out of true by the antimony-pencil. They were the mutinous sad eyes of some clumsy cartoon creature: a cartoon of animals dressed up and acting as human beings.

Narrator: She had indeed been brave enough to unveil, this stranger who sat facing him, staring at him with the painted eye one sees in frescoes with a forlorn and pitiable look of appeal. She wore an air of unsteady audacity as she confronted her lover, though her lips trembled and her large jowls shook with every vibration of the solid rubber tyres on the road. They stared at each other for a full two seconds before the darkness swallowed the light again. Then he raised her hand to his lips.

Mountolive: It was shaking like a leaf.

In the momentary light he had seen her uncombed and straggly hair hanging down the back of her neck, her thoughtless and disordered black dress. Her whole appearance had a rakish and improvised air. And the dark skin, so cruelly botched and cicatriced by the smallpox, looked coarse as the skin of an elephant. *He did not recognize her at all!* "Leila!" he cried.

Narrator: (It was almost a groan)

Mountolive: Pretending at last to identify and welcome the image of his lover

Narrator: (Now dissolved or shattered forever)

Mountolive: In this pitiable grotesque—a fattish Egyptian lady with all the marks of eccentricity and age written upon her appearance.

Narrator: Each time the lamps came up he looked again, and each time he saw himself confronting something like an animal cartoon figure—an elephant, say.

Mountolive: He could hardly pay attention to her words, so intent was he upon his racing feelings and memories.

Leila: I knew we should meet again some day. I knew it.

(She presses his hand, continuing to improvise under his speeches.)

Mountolive: She pressed his hand, and again he tasted her breath, heavy with sesame and mint and whisky.

Narrator: She was talking now and he listened uneasily, but with all the attention one gives to an unfamiliar language; and each time the street lamps came up to peer at them, he gazed at her anxiously—as if to see whether there had been any sudden magical change in her appearance. And then he was visited by another thought:

Mountolive: What if I too have changed as much as she has—if indeed this is she?

Narrator: What indeed? Sometime in the distant past they had exchanged images of one another like lockets; now his own had faded, changed. What might she see upon his face—

Mountolive: Traces of the feebleness which had overrun his youthful strength and purpose? He had now joined the ranks of those who compromise gracefully with life. Surely his ineffectuality, his unmanliness must be written all over his foolish, weak, good-looking face?

Narrator: He eyed her mournfully, with a pitiful eagerness to see whether she indeed really recognized him. He had forgotten that women will never surrender the image of their hearts' affections; no, she would remain forever blinded by the old love, refusing to let it be discountenanced by the new.

Leila: You have not changed by a day.

Narrator: Said this unknown woman with the disagreeable perfume.

Leila: My beloved, my darling, my angel. *(She continues to improvise under the speeches of Mountolive and the Narrator.)*

Mountolive: Mountolive flushed in the darkness at such endearments coming from the lips of an unknown personage.

Narrator: And the known Leila?

Mountolive: He suddenly realized that the precious image which had inhabited his heart for so long had now been dissolved, completely wiped out! He was suddenly face to face with the meaning of love and time. They had lost forever the power to fecundate each other's minds! He felt only self-pity and disgust where he should have felt love! And these feelings were simply not permissible. He swore at himself silently as they went up and down the dark causeway by the winter sea, like invalids taking the night air, their hands touching each other, in the old horse-drawn cab.

Narrator: She was talking faster, now, vaguely, jumping from topic to topic. Yet it all seemed an introduction to the central statement which she had come to make.

Leila: She was to leave tomorrow evening. Nessim's orders. Justine will come back from the lake and pick me up. We are disappearing together. At Kantara we'll separate and I shall go on to Kenya to the farm. Nessim won't say, can't say for how long as yet. I *had* to see you. I *had* to speak to you once. Not for myself—never for myself, my own heart. It was what I learned about Nessim at the carnival time. I was on the point of coming to meet you; but what he told me about

Palestine! My blood ran cold. To do something against the British! How could I! Nessim must have been mad. I didn't come because I would not have known what to say to you, how to face you. But now you know all.

Narrator: She had begun to draw her breath sharply now, to hurry onward as if all this were introductory matter to her main speech. Then suddenly she came out with it.

Leila: The Egyptians will harm Nessim, and the British are trying to provoke them to do so. David, you must use your power to stop it. I am asking you to save my son. I am asking you to save him. You must listen, must help me. I have never asked you a favour before. *(She continues to moan and plead under the Narrator's speech.)*

Narrator: *(Over the improvised speeches of Mountolive and Leila which become audible when the Narrator so indicates.)* The tear- and crayon-steaked face made her look even more of a stranger in the street-lights. He began to stammer. She cried aloud:

Leila: I implore you to help.

Narrator: And suddenly, to his intense humiliation, began to rock and moan like an Arab, pleading with him.

Mountolive: Leila, he cried, stop it!

Narrator: But she swayed from side to side, repeating the words, "Only you can save him now," more to herself, it seemed, than to anyone else. Then she showed some disposition to go down on her knees in the cab and kiss his feet. By this time Mountolive was trembling with anger and surprise and disgust. They were passing the Auberge for the tenth time.

Mountolive: Unless you stop at once—

Narrator: He cried angrily, but she wailed once more and he jumped awkwardly down into the road.

Mountolive: It was hateful to have to end their interview like this. He said, feeling stupid.

Narrator: And in a voice which seemed to come from far away and to have no recognizable expression save a certain old-fashioned waspishness:

Mountolive: *(To Leila)* I cannot discuss an official matter with a private person.

Narrator: Could anything be more absurd than these words?

Mountolive: He felt bitterly ashamed as he uttered them. "Leila, good-bye" he said hurriedly under his breath, and squeezed her hand once more before he turned.

Narrator: He took to his heels. He unlocked his car and climbed into it panting and overcome by a sense of ghastly folly. The cab moved off into the darkness.

Mountolive: He watched it curve slowly along the Corniche and disappear. Then he lit a cigarette and started his engine. All of a sudden there seemed nowhere in particular to go. Every impulse, every desire had faltered and faded out.

Narrator: After a long pause, he drove slowly and carefully back to the Summer Residence, talking to himself under his breath. The house was in darkness and he let himself in with his key. He walked from room to room switching on all the lights,

Mountolive: Feeling all of a sudden quite light-headed with loneliness; he could not accuse the servants of desertion since he had already told Ali that he would be dining out.

Narrator: But he walked up and down the drawing-room with his hands in his pockets for a long time.

Mountolive: He smelt the damp unheated rooms around him; the blank reproachful face of the clock told him that it was only just after nine.

Narrator: Abruptly, he went over to the cocktail cabinet and poured himself a very strong whisky and soda which he drank in one movement—gasping as if it were a dose of fruit salts.

Mountolive: His mind was humming now like a high-tension wire. He supposed that he would have to go out and have some dinner by himself.

Narrator: But where?

Mountolive: Suddenly the whole of Alexandria, the whole of Egypt, had become distasteful, burdensome, wearisome to his spirit.

Narrator: He drank several more whiskies, enjoying the warmth they brought to his blood—so unused was he to spirits which usually he drank very sparingly.

Mountolive: Leila had suddenly left him face to face with a reality which, he supposed, had always lain lurking behind the dusty tapestry of his romantic notions.

Narrator: In a sense, she had *been* Egypt, his own private Egypt of the mind; and now this old image had been husked, stripped bare.

Mountolive: "It would be intemperate to drink any more," he told himself as he drained his glass. Yes, that was it! He had never been intemperate, never been natural, outward-going in his attitude to life. He had always hidden behind measure and compromise;

Narrator: And this defection had somehow lost him the picture of the Egypt which had nourished him for so long.

Mountolive: Was it, then, all a lie?[13]

• • •

Although *The Alexandria Quartet* remains in some respects the fullest development of Durrell's favorite themes and images, his verse drama, *An Irish Faustus,* published in 1963, is one of his most compact statements of those images and themes.

This play, for all of its similarities to Marlowe's *Doctor Faustus,* is really quite different from its predecessor. As one critic has noted, "By the end of the play we have become aware that Durrell's real object has been the demolition not just of Marlowe's medieval Faustus or even of the medieval world, but the demolition of the medieval frame of mind which had invented a Faustus in the first place." [14] Durrell's Faustus, rather than being a necromancer, is a gentle moral philosopher who wants to live his life in peace and quiet. Unfortunately, he does have in his possession a ring of transmuted gold that could bring him all knowledge. Conflict does not occur for Faustus, however, until the ring is stolen.

The final irony in Durrell's play comes after Faustus' ring has been recovered, with the help of Mephisto. In the following scene, this irony becomes manifest as Durrell's Irish Faustus, determined to destroy the powerful ring, tricks, tempts, and coerces Mephisto into collaborating with him again.[15]

Scene Six. The cabinet of Dr. Faustus. Mephisto *is revealed sitting at ease before the fire, drinking wine. Enter* Faustus, *carefully locking and bolting the door.*

Faustus: Aha! So you are back again? I thought you would be.

Mephisto: Of course. And I thought it best to wait here for you, so I took the liberty of making myself at home.

Faustus: So I see.

Mephisto: You look tired, doctor.

Faustus: I am. Mortally tired.

Mephisto: You have recovered it, though—the ring I mean.

Faustus: Yes, I have recovered the ring.

Mephisto: You see? My information was correct.

Faustus: To the letter. I owe you a great debt.

Mephisto: Well, that is uncommonly graceful of you.

Faustus: Though perhaps not in the sense you imagine.

Mephisto: For restoring the ring, you mean?

Faustus: Not only that; for making me understand something
    Whose meaning has eluded me for years, . . .
    The problem of the ring and the problem of myself—
    They are one and the same thing.
    I can live with neither, I can rid myself of neither,
    Or at least it seemed so until now.

Mephisto: Elementary reasoning, doctor. You disappoint me.
    It's true that it cannot be done away with easily.
    It's true it represents a challenge you have not faced . . .

Faustus: Ah! There it is.

Mephisto: Faced with such a choice you could of course put it
    to use.
    Have you any inkling of its powers, man?
    Do you know what you hold in your hand?

Faustus: The temporal powers!

Mephisto: You talk like a prig or a parson—you, a scientist,
    Wedded to the quest for absolute truth in nature!
    It is astonishing. My good doctor, that is the gold,
    The alchemist's inmost secret, the veritable secret stone.
    From that you could make more, and more, and more, . . .
    The bottomless purse of Fortunatus is in your hand.
    Or else if you wish a whole new congeries of the sciences.
    They would be unlocked by the first convulsion of matter.

Faustus: Aye!

Mephisto: Think. All this power you could use for good!

Faustus: I am thinking of it. (Faustus *pours a drink,* Mephisto
    who misunderstands his ironic tone is much encouraged.
    He becomes cheerful.)

Mephisto: Good. Good. That is much better. My goodness me,
    There on your finger you have something to give you

Direct access to the prime material of earth,
The very bindings of the human soul, the wet clay of Adam!
This is not a parody of temporal power, as you say,
But a whole new world, of strange and wonderful proportions.
Everything you have known as power up to now is nothing
Compared to what lies slumbering in that ring
Aha there! I drink to your good fortune.

(Faustus *passes the crucifix into the hand which wears the*
ring in such a manner that the gesture is not lost upon the
audience. As he does so, Mephisto *suddenly shudders and*
puts down his glass with a bang.)

Faustus: What is it?

Mephisto: That chill again . . . that strange chill.

(*He stands up and looks around him.*)

Ah . . . It has passed . . .

Faustus: Strange to feel chilled before such a warm fire.

(Mephisto *recovers his composure.*)

Mephisto: Anyway, it has gone; let us refill the glasses.

(*As he does so he sees* Faustus *looking at him. He smiles*
and moves his head in a questioning gesture.)

What is it, doctor?

Faustus: Ah, my friend, now I know you; but how little as yet
You know me. We shall learn much from each other tonight.

Mephisto: I don't follow you.

Faustus: That will come.

Mephisto: There is something in your tone a little . . .
As if perhaps you did not trust me still.
Why? I have shown my good faith,
I have helped you to recover the ring have I not?

Faustus: Only to shackle me more firmly with it.

Mephisto: What *is* all this talk, man?

Faustus: I have come to set my purpose against yours.
I should have done it years ago, years ago.
You and I together are going to destroy the ring.

Mephisto: Destroy the . . .

(*He gazes at* Faustus *open-mouthed and then bursts into a*
peal of laughter.)

Destroy it? Do you know what you are saying?

Faustus: Yes I do.

Mephisto: My dear doctor! Let us talk sense.

Faustus. I am going to recite the Great Formula in a little while.

>   (Mephisto *springs up and stares uneasily at him. Then he laughs again.*)

Mephisto: The Great Formula! Would you dare to seek admission there?

>   My poor magician, you are mad. Besides it would not work!

Faustus: Yes, it always works if recited in the presence of one

>   Who comes from there, belongs there; do you see now?
>
>   I don't want to flatter you but you are an essential part
>
>   Of the experiment. I am sure it will be instructive.
>
>   Do you see? I need you as much as you need me!
>
>   (Mephisto *is uneasy now and out of countenance.*)

Mephisto: Enough of this argument, this preposterous idea.

>   No one has ever done it and escaped—you know as well as I.
>
>   You must be mad to think you can trick me.
>
>   The Great Formula indeed! You'd wither like a leaf!
>
>   No, no Faustus. I come here to help you
>
>   And this is all the thanks I get. How ungenerous!
>
>   If you go on like this I shall simply ask you give me back . . .

Faustus: The ring? But of course. You are most welcome. Take it.

>   (Faustus *holds out his hand and* Mephisto *tries to take it but finds that he is paralysed.*)

Mephisto: What is it? It dazzles me.

Faustus: Does something constrain you? Come, try again.

>   (Mephisto *is now thoroughly alarmed.*)

Mephisto: Faustus, what do you want of me, your friend?

>   Give me the ring and let me go;
>
>   I promise never to bother you again.

Faustus: Ah, no.

Mephisto: Surely you trust my word?

Faustus: No. Together we are going to burn the ring to ash.

Mephisto: You are mad. You are joking. Ha ha, you must be;

>   Well, I can take a joke as well as anyone.

Faustus: We will see if I am joking.

Mephisto: Faustus, listen to me for a moment.

Faustus: No. For once you listen to me. Come here. Sit down.

>   (With reluctant sullenness like a beaten dog Mephisto obeys.)
>
>   That is better.

Mephisto: You would never stand it, doctor, believe me.
    Your brain would shrivel, crack like a pod.
    The regions you speak of are . . . inhospitable to mortals. . . .
    Come, be sensible, give me the ring.
Faustus: I will, but at the right time; when we reach the place.
Mephisto: O foolish dabbler in what you do not know.
Faustus: I do not need to know. I imagine, therefore, I am free.
    How long it has taken me to understand that.
    Shall I describe the journey we must take
    Down to the slag heaps of nature's inmost processes,
    The threshing floor of time and matter?
Mephisto: Not there! Not there!
Faustus: Yes, there; the great molten heaps of unformed bodies,
    The carcass of the world's presumptuous hopes and fears,
    The matrix of creation's illness. . . . Yes.
    Prodigious vistas of terror and unreason
    Where volcanoes spout the blue blood of fire
    From all the severed arteries of time? The broken minds
    In heaps like spiders lying? The eternal smoke?
    The Alcahest we seek lies beyond the Ens Primum,
    Beyond the regions where only the deadly fictions thrive,
    Salamanders quivering in the white heart of pain,
    Caballi, lemures, the umbratiles of nightmare,
    Where the elementaries hooded like snakes shake out
    Ropes of white fire in coils . . . I know them all and
    Now that I know you I can face them all. O thank you,
    Mephisto! I thank you from the bottom of my mind.
Mephisto: I will not. I will not, I tell you.
    (Faustus *stands up triumphantly and raises his arms. As
    he begins to recite the Great Formula the stage slowly
    darkens.)*
Faustus: De divinibus operibus in secretis naturae . . .
Mephisto: Be warned, Faustus; be warned.
Faustus: De demonicis et obsessis, de sanguine ultra . . .
Mephisto: No. No further.
    (As Faustus *continues inexorably to recite, a wind rises
    almost drowning his voice. Then it falls again. There is a
    rolling of drums.* Mephisto *falls to his knees and backs
    away in terror.)*

I do not want to go back there; do not make me.
Master, I will do anything; I implore you. Please.
Listen, I have powers I never spoke of, great powers.
I would give you anything you wished. Let me go. Let me go.
(Faustus continues to recite. Mephisto is broken now.)
O if only God's charity had permitted us to die.
Do not take me back there Faustus; if you but knew
The loneliness, the spleen, the boredom.

Faustus: Come here and take my hand, poor fellow bondsman.
   (He drags the cowering Mephisto to his feet.)
   Veni, demonicis, Veni . . .

Mephisto: You will never come back, do you hear? Never. Never.
   You are killing reason; you will reverse the wheel
   Of cause and effect. Faustus, desist.
   *(His voice fades into the roaring of the wind. Objects fall and
   break. Suddenly with a crash of thunder the mouth of the
   pit opens with tongues of flame and white furnace light so
   bright that they both recoil. Then gathering courage Faustus
   begins to advance step by slow step, dragging the
   cringing Mephisto with him.)*[16]

• • •

"The Anecdotes: XVI, In Rio"

And so at last goodbye,
For time does not heed its own expenditure,
As the heart does in making old,
Infecting memory with a sigh-by-sigh,
Or the intolerable suppurating hope and wish.

It has no copy, moves in its own
Blind illumination seriously,
Traced somewhere perhaps by a yellow philosopher
Motionless over a swanpan,
Who found the door open—it always is:
Who found the fire banked: it never goes out.

We, my dear Melissa, are only typics of
This Graeco-Roman asylum, dedicated here
To an age of Bogue, where the will sticks
Like a thorn under the tongue,
Making our accent pain and not completeness.

Do not interrupt me . . . Let me finish:
Madmen established in the intellect

By the domestic error of a mind that arranges,
Explains, but can never sufficiently include:
Punishes, exclaims, but never completes its arc
To enter the Round. Nor all the cabals
Of pity and endurance in the circus of art
Will change it till the mainspring will is broken.

Yet the thing can be done, as you say, simply
By sitting and waiting, the mystical leap
Is only a figure for it, it involves not daring
But the patience, being gored, not to cry out.
But perhaps even the desire itself is dying.
I should like that: to make an end of it.

It is time we did away with this kind of suffering,
It has become a pose and refuge for the lazy:
As for me I must do as I was born
And so must you: upon the smaller part of the circle
We desire fulfilment in the measure of our gift:

You kiss and make: while I withdraw and plead.[17]

The Production

Obviously the first problem posed by a composite program such as "Cities, Plains, and People" is the selection of literature to be included in the program. Since the object of this Readers Theatre presentation was to provide the audience with a composite view of the many facets of Durrell, the man and the artist, literature was selected that would be indicative of Durrell's range of artistic expression and that would provide some continuity between Durrell's personal and literary lives. Consequently, the material selected ranged from Durrell's imaginative works, such as his novels, lyric poems, and plays, to his nonfictional travel books and his personal correspondence with Henry Miller. The transitional comments between some of the selections had the purpose of clarifying for the audience a particular work's place in the total view of Durrell.

Eight performers—five men and three women—were used in the production. The use of the casting principles explored in Chapter Three allowed one actor to be used to play several similar roles (that is, similar aspects of Durrell), and also allowed more than one actor to play the same role. Not only could more than one actor play the "Durrell character," but also, as can be seen from the script, two actors were occasionally used to play the same persona in a given selection, in order to indicate differences within that persona. Furthermore, the use of male and female actors allowed for a demonstration of the bisexual nature of the persona in certain selections. For example, not only did one of the women portray the homosexual Balthazar and the emotionally adolescent Darley in *The Alexandria Quartet,* but also, a man and a woman were used to play the two Durrells in the passage from *Bitter Lemons.*

An interesting side effect of the casting was that, because all of the actors at some time portrayed Durrell (or his persona), there was a clear sense of seeing many faces of Durrell; and yet, because these actors were also playing non-Durrell roles (for example, they all handled transitional pieces of criticism), there was also a sense that Durrell himself was a much larger force than any one of the actors alone could embody.

The staging of "Cities, Plains, and People," because it was founded on the principles of line direction and movement discussed in Chapter Four, was relatively simple. Cues were taken from the individual texts, and presentational and representational staging were used alternately, according to what was required by the specific selections. Furthermore, it was found that by using the principles of visually perceived movement discussed earlier, the effect of a large amount of movement could be accomplished with a minimum of actual motion. This was particularly relevant in the passages from *Bitter Lemons, Mountolive,* and *An Irish Faustus.*

Because of the nature of the script, the costumes, properties, and settings for "Cities, Plains, and People" had to accomplish two purposes: they *usually* had to generalize rather than particularize, and they had to relate to the whole text as well as the individual selections. The costumes chosen were essentially "rehearsal clothes," which would negate any literalizing of the costumes for characters and would encourage alienation by calling attention to the actors as actors. These rehearsal clothes consisted of bright Mediterranean blue and green shirts, turtleneck sweaters, and khaki slacks. Such costuming had the effect, through its bright colors and style, of paralleling much of the rich casualness of the cities, plains, and people that are the subjects of Durrell's writings. To these basic costumes were then added literalized costume pieces for specific characters in specific scenes, when this was called for by the text. For example, Leila in *Mountolive* is clothed in a long black dress and veil; these costume pieces were put on (in full view of the audience, again to encourage alienation) over the actress' basic costume.

Generally speaking, these properties that were particularized in the texts (such as Faustus' crucifix) were literalized in the production, and those that were generalized in the texts (such as the milk and croissants in *Bitter Lemons*) were suggested through pantomime. However, some attention should be given to the use of one traditional Readers Theatre prop: the manuscript. To begin with, all of the actors had manuscripts at some time during the production, in order to encourage alienation. These manuscripts were also used to underscore the differences between written and spoken style in the various selections, as well as the differences between set speeches and spontaneous speeches. The manuscripts were not used when the actors' characters seemed to speak spontaneously, as for example in Mephisto's unprepared response to Faustus' demands, and Leila's disconnected and rambling pleas to Mountolive.

In addition to being used for their alienation effect, manuscripts were frequently used to underline the differences between the text that was already written and the text that was still in the process of being written. To indicate this difference, the actors would occasionally write rather than read or speak their texts, in order to parallel the writing process that characterizes several of the selections. Indeed, the actress playing Darley in *The Alexandria Quartet* even wrote her passage from *Justine* with a baroque quill pen, which served as a visual counterpart to the text's baroque verbal style. On another occasion, when Durrell writes to Henry Miller of his inability to write anything worthwhile, the actor playing Durrell silently read through a page of his manuscript, threw it down in disgust and walked away from it. At this point, one of the other actors picked up the discarded manuscript and proceeded to read from it Durrell's poem "Alexandria." Here the manuscript of the poem served as a bridge between the agonies of creation and the created poem. In short, then, it seemed quite possible in this production to utilize the manuscripts of the particular texts in order to clarify or provide insights into the structure or texture of the individual selections as well as the text of the entire program.

Because of the fast shifts from generalized to specified settings in "Cities, Plains, and People," a flexible setting was a necessity. Consequently, the setting consisted essentially of a unit set of levels, platforms, and a ramp, to which could be added the necessary pieces of furniture when a specific setting (such as Faustus' room) would be required. For example, in accord with the principle discussed in Chapter Five, a large heavy lectern was added for the scene from *An Irish Faustus*, in order to underline the shifting restrictions that occur in Mephisto and Faustus. Two other set pieces used in this production were a prop table and a costume rack. While these set pieces obviously served a practical purpose, their more important aesthetic and critical function was to encourage alienation simply through their presence on stage.

Additional technical aspects of the production, such as lighting and sound, were also relatively simple. Generally speaking, the lighting of the actors and the stage area was designed essentially to support the mood of each individual selection, with special spots being used to parallel particular points of focus in a given scene. Although general lighting was not used throughout the production, it should be pointed out that there was always enough illumination on all of the actors so that they could all be seen all of the time. This, again, was done to encourage alienation. Only one special lighting effect was used, at the end of the scene from *An Irish Faustus*. Here, in order to achieve the effects the text's nonliteralized scene, a lobsterscope was used in conjunction with sound effects to suggest the horrific effects on Faustus and Mephisto of the opening of the lower depths. In addition to the lighting on stage, the degree of lighting in the audience area shifted throughout the production. These shifts, in accord with the principle of audience lighting discussed in Chapter Five, were determined by the degree of audience participation implied in the individual portions of the text.

Very little mechanical sound was used in the production.

Greek and Levantine music was played for the entrance and exit of the actors and during some of the major transitions in the script, in order to provide an appropriate nonverbal musical setting for Durrell and his works. Furthermore, the first poem in the script, "Bitter Lemons," was a recorded reading of the poem by Durrell himself. This use of Durrell's own reading was an attempt to present the audience with not only the imagined and personated voice of Durrell that is present in his works, but also the actual voice of the poet himself.

A final word should be said about the relationship of the performers to the text. Because of the extensive employment of alienation in this production, and because each of the actors was required to play several characters in the text, it was most important that the actors not only learn how to express their respective characters, but also that they clarify their roles as actors. That is, the actors had to study their characters' expressions as well as their expression of themselves as actors. This is particularly necessary in a production that is using alienation effects, because the audience must be able to distinguish between actor and character when such a distinction is demanded. If it seems to some readers that alienation is receiving undue emphasis in this discussion, it should be remembered that if Readers Theatre is to be a valuable critical tool in the study of literature, then alienation is of central importance in accomplishing this goal.

Throughout this discussion, I have obviously only touched on some of the problems and their solutions found in one particular production. Nonetheless, this discussion, combined with the discussions in the preceding chapters, will perhaps alert the Readers Theatre director to the possibilities inherent in a kind of theatre that is interested in featuring a literary text. And, as has been repeatedly maintained, in order to achieve this kind of theatre, we must begin to develop a workable aesthetic to serve as our guide. It is hoped that the principles explored throughout this book may provide such a beginning toward finding a grammar of practice for Readers Theatre.

Notes

Chapter Two

1. "Perspective Interview: Kenneth Tynan with Studs Terkel," *Perspective on Ideas and the Arts,* 12 (June 1963), 16.
2. For a full discussion of the special problems encountered in staging narrative literature, see Robert S. Breen, "Chamber Theatre," unpublished manuscript, copyright Evanston, Illinois, 1964. Mimeographed.

Chapter Four

1. Richard Brinsley Sheridan, "The School for Scandal," in Lynn Altenbernd and Leslie L. Lewis (eds.), *Introduction to Literature: Plays* (New York: Macmillan, 1963), p. 142.
2. Eudora Welty, "Why I Live at the P. O.," in Albert Erskine and Robert Penn Warren (eds.), *Short Story Masterpieces* (New York: Dell Laurel Edition, 1958), p. 534.
3. Oscar Wilde, "The Importance of Being Earnest," in Joseph Satin (ed.), *Reading Drama* (Boston: Houghton Mifflin, 1964), pp. 849–850.
4. J. D. Salinger, *The Catcher in the Rye* (Boston: Little, Brown, 1951), pp. 52–53.
5. Rudolph Arnheim, *Art and Visual Perception: A Psychology of the Creative Eye* (Berkeley: University of California Press, 1965). See especially Chapter VIII, "Movement," for a full discussion of the theories of visual perception discussed here.
6. *Ibid.,* pp. 396–424.
7. *Ibid.,* p. 417.
8. *Ibid.,* pp. 360–361.
9. *Ibid.,* p. 365.

10. *Ibid.*, pp. 366 ff. See also Karl Dunker, "In Motion," in Willis D. Ellis (ed.), *A Source Book of Gestalt Psychology* (New York: Harcourt, Brace & World, 1939).

11. Arnheim, *op. cit.*, p. 366.

12. *Ibid.*

13. *Ibid.*, pp. 372–373.

14. Flannery O'Connor, *Everything That Rises Must Converge* (New York: Farrar, Straus & Giroux, 1965), pp. 85–89.

15. Albert Camus, *The Stranger* (New York: Vintage Books, 1946), p. 75.

16. *Ibid.*

17. Arnheim, *op. cit.*, p. 368.

18. *Ibid.*

19. *Ibid.*, pp. 382–385.

20. *Ibid.*, p. 382.

21. *Ibid.*

22. *Ibid.*, p. 407.

23. For a full discussion of alienation, see Bertolt Brecht, *Brecht on Theatre*, ed. and trans. John Willett(New York: Hill and Wang, 1964).

24. Nelson Algren, "A Bottle of Milk for Mother," in Albert Erskine and Robert Penn Warren (eds.), *Short Story Masterpieces* (New York: Dell Laurel Edition, 1958), pp. 43–44.

Chapter Five

1. Dylan Thomas, *Adventures in the Skin Trade* (New York: New Directions, 1955).

2. *Ibid.*, pp. 52–55. Chamber Theatre adaptation by Joseph E. Conaway.

3. Thomas, *op. cit.*, p. 36.

4. For a full discussion of this social aspect of the self, see Erving Goffman, *The Presentation of Self in Everyday Life* (Garden City, N. Y.: Doubleday, 1959).

5. Marshall McLuhan, *The Gutenberg Galaxy* (Toronto: University of Toronto Press, 1965), pp. 96 ff.

6. Rudolph Arnheim, *Art and Visual Perception: A Psychology of the Creative Eye* (Berkeley: University of California Press, 1965), pp. 398–403. See also Wassily Kandinsky, *Point and Line to Plane*, ed. Hilla Rebay, trans. Howard Dearstyne and Hilla Rebay (New York: The Solomon R. Guggenheim Foundation for the Museum of Non-Objective Painting, 1947).

7. Arnheim, *op. cit.*, p. 402.

8. *Ibid.*, p. 403.

9. *Ibid.*, p. 411.

10. *Ibid.*, p. 410.

11. For standard discussions on problems and solutions in stage lighting, see Theodore Fuchs, *Stage Lighting* (Boston: Little, Brown, 1929), and Samuel Selden and Hunton D. Sellman, *Stage Scenery and Lighting*, 3rd ed. (New York: Appleton-Century-Crofts, 1959).

12. For a fuller discussion of the effects of this production on the audience, see Robert Brustein, "A Night in the Brig," *The New Republic*, 148 (June 1, 1963), 28–29.

13. Robert Bolt, *A Man For All Seasons* (New York: Random House, 1962), pp. vii–xx.

Chapter Six

1. Henri Bergson, *Laughter: An Essay on the Meaning of the Comic*, trans. Cloudesley Bereton and Fred Rothwell (New York: Macmillan, 1937).

2. Rudolph Arnheim, *Art and Visual Perception: A Psychology of the Creative Eye* (Berkeley: University of California Press, 1965), p. 393.

3. *Ibid.*

Chapter Seven

1. Lawrence Durrell, "Bitter Lemons," in *The Poetry of Lawrence Durrell* (New York: Dutton, 1962), p. 29.

2. Derek Stanford, "Lawrence Durrell: An Early View of His Poetry," in Harry T. Moore (ed.), *The World of Lawrence Durrell* (Carbondale: Southern Illinois University Press, 1962), p. 38.

3. George Wickes (ed.), *Lawrence Durrell and Henry Miller: A Private Correspondence* (New York: Dutton, 1963), p. 59.

4. Durrell, "Cities, Plains, and People, I," *The Poetry of Lawrence Durrell, op. cit.*, pp. 134–135.

5. Lawrence Durrell, *Bitter Lemons* (New York: Dutton, 1958), pp. 15–17. Chamber Theatre adaptation mine.

6. Lawrence Durrell, *Prospero's Cell and Reflections on a Marine Venus* (New York: Dutton, 1962), p. 11.

7. Durrell, "Exile in Athens," *The Poetry of Lawrence Durrell, op. cit.*, p. 45.

8. Wickes, *op. cit.*, pp. 167–168.

9. *Ibid.*, pp. 186–188.

10. Lawrence Durrell, "Alexandria," *Selected Poems* (New York: Grove, 1957), pp. 59–60.

11. Lawrence Durrell, *The Alexandria Quartet* (New York: Dutton, 1962), p. 17.

12. *Ibid.*, p. 210.

13. *Ibid.*, pp. 618–623. Chamber Theatre adaptation mine.

14. John Unterecker, "Lawrence Durrell," Columbia Essays on Modern Writers, No. 6 (New York: Columbia University Press, 1964), p. 33.

15. *Ibid.*, pp. 32–34.

16. Lawrence Durrell, *An Irish Faustus* (New York: Dutton, 1963), pp. 59–74.

17. Durrell, "The Anecdotes: XVI, In Rio," *The Poetry of Lawrence Durrell, op. cit.*, pp. 79–80.

Index

A

B

Readers Theatre Class